Eq

THEMES FOR THE 21ST CENTURY

Titles in this series

Equality

ALEX CALLINICOS

Polity

First published in 2000 by Polity Press in association with Blackwell Publishers Ltd

Editorial office:
Polity Press
65 Bridge Street
Cambridge CB2 1UR, UK

Marketing and production:
Blackwell Publishers Ltd
108 Cowley Road
Oxford OX4 1JF, UK

Published in the USA by
Blackwell Publishers Inc.
Commerce Place
350 Main Street
Malden, MA 02148, USA

A catalogue record for this book is available from the British Library.

Library of Congress Cataloging-in-Publication Data
Callinicos, Alex.
   Equality / Alex Callinicos.
      p. cm.
   Includes bibliographical references and index.
   ISBN 0-7456-2324-7 (acid-free paper) — ISBN 0-7456-2325-5 (pbk. : acid-free paper)
   1. Equality.   I. Title.
JC575 .C36 2000
320'.01'1–dc21   00-025853

Typeset in 10.5 on 12 pt Plantin
by SetSystems, Saffron Walden, Essex
Printed in Great Britain by T. J. International, Padstow, Cornwall

This book is printed on acid-free paper.

In Memoriam

Margaret Acton
(1919–1997)

Pelline Eyre
(1906–1998)

Contents

Preface and Acknowledgements

In venturing incautiously into the domain of normative political theory, I have incurred some major debts. For nearly twenty years now I have been a fellow traveller with a very lively community of political philosophers at the University of York. At least some of their understanding of the deep issues raised by the idea of social justice must have rubbed off on me and may therefore be reflected (no doubt in distorted form) in this book. My general thinking about equality has been greatly influenced by the work of three other philosophers – Etienne Balibar, Jacques Bidet and Jerry Cohen. I share with them a common background in the Marxist tradition – though I am sure they would all think me much too orthodox. I have also learned from the MA students who, over the years, have asked me to supervise dissertations devoted to the relationship between Marx and Rawls.

David Held must share some responsibility for this book, since he suggested – while I was still reeling with exhaustion from the effort of executing another of his commissions – that I write it, and has offered much helpful editorial guidance once I had succumbed to his blandishments. David, along with Tony Giddens and John Thompson, is to be congratulated for developing in Polity a publishing house where social and political theorists of often radically (and sometimes increasingly) divergent views can flourish. I am also grateful to others at Polity – Sandra Byatt, Louise Knight and Pam Thomas – and to Chris Bessant, for making the process of producing this book as smooth and painless as possible.

Sam Ashman and an anonymous referee read and commented on my manuscript in draft. Chapter 3, the philosophical core of the book, was presented as a paper at the Political Theory Workshop at York. Though sinking with flu, I found the discussion very helpful; Matt Matravers (who has also been an invaluable source of arguments and references) and Sue Mendus went beyond the call of duty to provide me with their written comments. I would like to thank them all: no doubt if I had taken their criticisms as seriously as I should have, this would have been a better book.

Equality is dedicated to the memory of two beloved aunts. There is much bad luck in the world, but I am very fortunate to have known them.

1

Inequality Today

A world of inequality

Rich beyond the wildest imaginings of earlier generations, the world enters the twenty-first century heaving with poverty and inequality. The United Nations Development Programme (UNDP) produces an annual *Human Development Report* largely devoted to the melancholy task of documenting the steady growth in global social and economic inequality. According to the 1999 report, the ratio of the income of the richest fifth of the world's population to that of the poorest fifth had risen from 30 to 1 in 1960 to 60 to 1 in 1990. By 1997 the ratio had risen to 74 to 1.[1]

In its most headline grabbing aspect, the *Human Development Report* plots the progress of the super-rich. Between 1994 and 1998 the richest 200 people in the world more than doubled their net worth, from $440 to $1,042 billion: the latter sum was equivalent to the income of 41 per cent of the world's population. During the same period, the number of people who must live on less than one US dollar a day remained unchanged at 1.3 billion. Between them, Bill Gates, the Walton family (owners of the Walmart supermarket chain) and the Sultan of Brunei were worth the combined national income of the 36 least developed countries in the world.[2]

Inequality is not simply a literally global problem that divides the rich North from the poor South. Inequalities within individual countries are also growing. According to the UNDP, the transition to market capitalism in eastern Europe and the former Soviet Union produced 'the fastest rise in inequality ever. Russia now has the greatest inequality – the income share of the richest 20 per cent is 11 times that of the poorest 20 per cent.' Between 1987–8 and 1993–5 the Gini coefficient measuring inequality rose in Russia at an incredible rate from 0.24 to 0.48. In Latin America, despite the sporadic waves of euphoria that swept financial markets over the region's resumption of economic growth after the 1980s debt crisis, the Gini coefficient remained stable at 0.58.[3]

A much more vivid, and more heart-breaking, indication of the realities of global inequality than all these statistics was provided by the case of Yaguine Koita and Fodé Tounkara. At the beginning of August 1999 these two teenagers from Guinea-Conakry were found dead of cold and asphyxiation in the undercarriage of an airliner at Brussels airport. A letter found on their bodies explained their desperate and fatal flight. It read in part:

... Your Excellencies the members and leaders of Europe,

We have the honourable pleasure and the great confidence to write this letter to speak to you about the objective of our journey and the suffering of us, the children and young people of Africa ... It is to your solidarity and your kindness that we appeal for help in Africa. Help us, we suffer enormously in Africa, help us we have problems and some lack of rights for children ... Thus, if you see that we have sacrificed ourselves and risked our lives, it is because people suffer too much in Africa and because we need you to fight against poverty and war in Africa. Nevertheless, we want to study, and we ask you to help us study to become like you in Africa. Finally, we beg you to forgive us very firmly for having dared to write this letter to such great personages as yourselves, to whom we owe much respect . . .[4]

The great personages of Europe paused briefly to shed a tear for the boys before returning to their usual business of denying refugees and 'economic migrants' access to their countries.

Poverty and inequality in the advanced economies

The gap between rich and poor has been growing in the advanced economies themselves. Out of nineteen OECD countries, only one saw inequalities in earnings and income fall during the 1980s and early 1990s.[5] In the United States, it has often been neo-conservative commentators who have been quickest to note the trend. At the end of the 1980s, the Republican political analyst Kevin Phillips documented the systematic efforts of Ronald Reagan's two administrations to redistribute wealth and income from the poor to the rich. Calling the 1980s a new Gilded Era, he contended: 'No parallel upsurge of riches had been seen since the late nineteenth century, the era of Vanderbilts, Morgans and Rockefellers.'[6]

A decade later, the Washington-based strategy consultant Edward Luttwak traced the further development of this process, which he saw as a consequence of the development of a new, uncontrolled 'turbo-capitalism':

The United States is on its way to acquiring the income-distribution characteristics of a Third World country, with a truly very rich top 1 per cent, and a significant minority (roughly 12 per cent) which remains below the official poverty line even though fully employed, forty hours a week, fifty weeks a year. In New York State, whose economy is very dynamic and especially turbo-capitalist – it contains Wall Street, after all – income distribution has predictably become even more unequal than in the United States as a whole. In 1996 the average income of the richest one-fifth of all households was almost twenty times higher at $132,390 than that of the poorest fifth at $6,787. Only in Washington DC was the ratio even more extreme at 28.2, while the averages for the United States as a whole were $117,499 and $9,254, a ratio of 12.7. In New York State, moreover, the average income of the top-earning fifth of all households increased by 46 per cent between 1978 and 1996, while that of the poorest fifth of all households declined by 36 per cent.[7]

Britain – the major economy to have followed the US most closely in its trajectory towards deregulated free-market capitalism during the 1980s and 1990s – displayed a similar pattern. The New Labour government elected in May 1997 is – as we shall see in subsequent chapters – at best equivocal in its pursuit of greater equality, but research into the causes of and remedies for poverty and inequality has flourished under the patronage of the ambitious Chancellor of the Exchequer, Gordon Brown. According to this research, inequality in the distribution of income, measured by the Gini coefficient, rose by a third between 1977 and 1996–7. This reflected, *inter alia*, a growing earnings gap – for men, earnings in the top decile of the workforce rose twice as fast as those in the bottom decile, for women four times as fast – and a rise in the proportion of workless households from 9 per cent in 1979 to 20 per cent in 1995–6.[8]

The detailed studies on which these conclusions were based tend to challenge the idea put forward by neo-

liberal apologists for the policies of the Reagan–Thatcher
era that increased income inequalities are compensated
for by growing job-market mobility, allowing talented and
thrusting individuals to climb the economic ladder:

> The pattern of year-to-year mobility . . . can be summa-
> rized in terms of what I label the 'rubber-band' model of
> income dynamics. One may think of each person's income
> fluctuating around a relatively fixed 'longer-term average'.
> This value is a tether on the income scale to which people
> are attached by a rubber band. They may move away from
> the tether from one year to the next, but not too far because
> of the band holding them. And they tend to rebound back
> towards and around the tether over a period of several
> years.[9]

The studies also contradict the view taken by defenders of
the Anglo-American variant of liberal capitalism that the
relatively high proportion of low-paid jobs in the US and
Britain offer their incumbents both secure employment
and the prospect of economic advancement:

> There is strong evidence of a cycle of low pay and no pay.
> The low-paid are more likely to be out of work in the
> future; those out of work are more likely to be low-paid on
> re-entry; and are even more likely to be so if they had been
> low-paid prior to being out of work.
>   The hypothesis that low-paid jobs act as stepping-stones
> to higher paid jobs is not supported by the data. The
> evidence presented here suggests that low-paid jobs are
> more likely to act as blind alleys than as stepping-stones to
> positions higher up the pay distribution.[10]

Blind alleys in which the low-paid are trapped, rubber
bands tethering us to our places in the income structure:
these metaphors hardly offer reassuring images of the
'labour flexibility' which even centre-left politicians claim

among the chief merits of the Anglo-Saxon *laissez-faire* economies. A third Treasury-commissioned paper summarizes the evidence for wage mobility in Britain somewhat more formally:

> the picture that is sometimes painted of a mobile society is far from the truth. In fact, the evidence shows a high degree of immobility with little long-range wage movements. In addition to this there is evidence showing that earnings mobility has fallen since the late 1970s. Given that we have also seen a sharp rise in cross sectional wage inequality [i.e. the overall distribution of earnings as opposed to individuals' movement from one place in this distribution to another] over this time period, this tells us that not only has the gap between rich and poor risen but the ability of the low-paid to close this gap has fallen considerably. Far from offsetting the increase in cross section wage inequality, changes in mobility appears [*sic*] to have exacerbated this rise.[11]

What is revealed in these studies is an embedded structure of inequality:

> Although children frequently do end up in a different economic position to their parents, for most people the movement is short-range. This is particularly true of children from advantaged backgrounds. Children with advantaged parents are very likely to end up advantaged themselves . . . around 80 per cent of boys whose fathers were in the top quarter of the earnings distribution end up in the top half of the earnings distribution. But the chances of ending up in the top half of the earnings distribution are much lower for boys whose fathers were in the poorest quarter. Just over a third of the boys with parents in the bottom quarter manage to move up to the top half of the earnings distribution. The pattern of mobility is not significantly different for girls.[12]

Studies such as the ones just cited quite legitimately tend to concentrate on poverty and inequality as problems afflicting the worst-off minority of the population. But broader discussions often proceed on the assumption that the growth in inequality documented above is one that pits an affluent majority against an impoverished minority, the latter frequently stereotyped as an 'underclass' trapped in a whole complex of deviant behaviours. Even egalitarian philosophers often appear to share this belief. For example, Thomas Nagel writes: 'As things are, democracy is the enemy of comprehensive equality, once the poor cease to be a majority.'[13] Essentially the same view is at the heart of the 'Third Way' political strategy pursued by Bill Clinton in the United States and by social-democratic leaders such as Tony Blair and Gerhard Schröder in the European Union: since the poor constitute only a minority of the electorate, the centre left must avoid redistributive policies that might antagonize the affluent majority.

What is surprising about this very widely held belief is that those who accept it rarely seem to engage with the very considerable evidence contradicting it. The problem is partly a conceptual one. The concepts of equality and inequality are plainly relational: one can only establish the degree to which either obtains by comparing different individuals' access to the relevant advantages (the correct basis on which to make such interpersonal comparisons is one of the main themes of chapter 3 below).[14] But even some egalitarians are unwilling to conceive poverty also in relational terms. Thus G.A. Cohen writes: 'By plausible absolute standards, most people in the past were poor, and the target for redistribution could then be a rich minority. Now, by the same absolute standards, the standards in the light of which it is pertinently pointed out that 62 per cent of UK households have videos, only a minority are poor.'[15]

But this seems much too quick. One can certainly identify a set of biologically determined basic subsistence needs the failure to meet which represents a benchmark of absolute poverty. But the criteria for meeting these basic needs are likely to change according to the standards prevailing in the society in question. For example, few would accept that what a medieval peasant would regard as adequate housing can count as meeting the basic need for shelter at the beginning of the twenty-first century: the fact that a huge segment of the world's population are forced to live in shacks and hovels that might once have seemed acceptable is now treated as evidence of the extent of poverty today.

Moreover, there are also needs that do not reflect the transhistorical invariants of human existence but whose fulfilment may be a necessary condition of living an adequate life in a given society. To lack access to a telephone, television, or safe and efficient transport is to be fundamentally disadvantaged in contemporary urban civilization. Technological change may make much more complex consumer durables a crucial resource for living an adequate life. Amid all the hype surrounding the internet and the world-wide web, the UNDP points out that in 1998 a tiny – generally affluent, educated and male – 2.4 per cent of the world's population used the internet.[16] How long before lack of access to a personal computer with a modem becomes the basis of a new form of disadvantage?

These considerations suggest that poverty, like equality itself, should be conceptualized in relational terms. Such indeed is in many cases already the practice. For example, in official British statistics the poor are defined as those living on a household income below 50 per cent of the national average (after housing costs). In 1996/7, 14 million people, nearly a quarter of the population of the

United Kingdom, fell under this definition of poverty, compared to only 4 million in 1979.[17]

This growth in the numbers of the poor contrasts with rising *average* incomes. In 1999, average earnings for full-time British workers reached £20,265, a figure that certainly seems to support the image of a 'contented' majority.[18] Averages are, however, often misleading: in an economy where the income of the better off has been increasing much faster than that of the worse off, average earnings may rise without the relative position of the majority necessarily improving. In 1994/5 63 per cent of the UK population received a net household disposable income that was below the average: yet again this represented a rise compared to 1979, when 59 per cent of the population were on below-average incomes.[19]

These figures suggest only a deterioration in the *relative* position of the majority, in Britain at least. A sufficiently robust rise in absolute living standards could still leave this majority enjoying considerably greater material comforts than they did a generation ago – and indeed such is the picture evoked by surveys that document the steady rise in household ownership of a wide variety of consumer durables many of which (such as video recorders and personal computers) did not exist thirty or forty years ago. A rising tide lifts all boats, as John F. Kennedy once put it.

Yet, despite this profusion of new products for the mass market, the greatest capitalist economy of them all, the United States, presents a very different case, one where living standards have come under constant *downward* pressure over the past generation. This fact – which has, astonishingly, gone largely ignored in both political and theoretical debates – has nevertheless been thoroughly documented and analysed by commentators and researchers of different political persuasions. Thus the neo-conservative Luttwak writes:

Measured in constant 1982 dollars, the average earnings of all 'non-supervisory' American employees working in all industries and all services, other than agriculture or government, peaked in 1978 at $8.40 an hour, only to decline to $7.78 in 1980, $7.77 in 1985 and $7.52 in 1990, finally increasing during the post-1993 boom, but even then only by very little and very slowly, from $7.50 in 1996 to $7.66 in 1997.[20]

The Marxist historian Robert Brenner presents a similar picture in his monumental study of post-war capitalism:

Between 1979 and 1990, real hourly compensation in the [US] private business economy grew at an average rate of 0.1 per cent. The trend in these years for hourly real wages and salaries (excluding benefits) was far worse, *falling* at an average rate of 1 per cent. At no time previously in the twentieth century had real wage growth been anywhere so low for anywhere so long.[21]

So too does the economic journalist Jeffrey Madrick from a left-liberal perspective:

As a result of these factors, the average real income of families was only a few percentage points higher in 1993 than in 1973, and that largely because so many more spouses were working. There have been shorter periods when wages have fallen sharply, but as far as we can tell, there has been no other twenty-year period since 1820 when average real wages fell, with the possible exception of the years just before and after the Civil War.[22]

Madrick goes on to document the consequences of what Brenner describes as this 'repression of wages' – a longer working year, up by a week and a half since 1973, for full-time male employees; the largest increase in the proportion of working spouses in the poorest households, suggesting that many women entered the labour market not in search of 'empowerment' but driven by financial hardship; a decline in home ownership among the young; a fall also in the number of cars purchased per worker as Detroit shifted towards producing luxury vehicles such as light trucks for the affluent middle class; shrinking proportions of employees covered by private pension and health insurance schemes. 'In general,' he concludes, 'America is evolving into a two-tier society, and the upper tier is shrinking.'[23]

Remarkably then, in an era proclaimed as marking the definitive triumph of liberal capitalism over the systemic challenge represented by socialism and communism, the working majority in the most powerful economy in the world experienced, perhaps for the first time, something resembling what Marx called 'absolute impoverishment'. Elsewhere in the advanced societies the picture is less stark. Nevertheless, the same processes are at work, as the relentless drive to reduce costs in the face of international competition places the jobs, wages and conditions of the bulk of the working population under constant pressure.

One leading social-democratic economist, Will Hutton, has summed up the consequences of this process in Britain during the Tory years: 'more than half the people who are eligible to work are living either on poverty incomes or in conditions of permanent stress and insecurity'. He divides the working population into three groups. 'The first 30 per cent are the *disadvantaged* – the unemployed, those on government schemes and the like. 'The second 30 per cent are made up of the *marginalized* and the *insecure*. This category is defined not so much by incomes as by its relation to the labour market.' Those falling under it 'work at jobs that are insecure, poorly protected and carry few benefits. This category more than any other is at the receiving end of the changes blowing around Britain's offices and factories; it includes the growing number of part-timers and casual workers.' Finally, there are 'the *privileged* – the just over 40 per cent whose market power has grown since 1979'.[24]

The picture Hutton paints is, if anything, too optimistic since he includes in the category of 'the privileged' those full-time employees who have held their positions for more than two years: many of these have come under intense pressure as a result of the sustained efforts to restructure both public and private bureaucracies along more profitable lines. Indeed, the sociologist Pierre Bourdieu argues that various developments – among them, chronic mass unemployment, the growth in contract labour and flexible production, and 'the *deterritorialization of the enterprise*' now freed from any specific attachment to region or nation – mean that 'insecurity [*précarité*] is everywhere today': 'Objective insecurity supports a generalized subjective insecurity which today affects, at the heart of an advanced economy, the majority of the workers and even those who are not or not yet directly hit.' Indeed, this is part of 'a *mode of domination* of a new type, based on the institution of a generalized and permanent condition of insecurity aiming to compel the workers to submission, to the acceptance of exploitation'.[25]

Does inequality matter?

With these remarks of Bourdieu's we plainly move beyond the facts of inequality today to our moral and political response to them. For some these facts require the kind of interpretation present in Nagel's observation that '[w]e live in a world of spiritually sickening economic and social inequality, a world whose progress toward the acknowledgement of common standards of toleration, individual liberty and human development has been depressingly slow and unsteady.'[26]

But, of course, many would reject such an interpretation. For the neo-liberal defenders of unrestrained capitalism, the inequalities found in the advanced countries at least are largely the consequence of individuals' free choices over the use of their talents and resources in a market economy. As has been most forcefully argued by Robert Nozick in *Anarchy, State, and Utopia,* the resulting differences in wealth and income do not constitute an injustice requiring political action to remedy it. Neo-liberals tend to interpret the residual inequalities that they do not believe can be explained in these terms as the perverse effects of statist attempts to interfere in the workings of the market. For some, among them adherents to the New Right as well as supporters of more traditional conservative views, the persistent inequality between black and white that so scars American society in particular is to be explained by genetic differences which, they claim, underlie African-Americans' poor performance in intelligence tests.

It is hardly surprising that the political right should seek either to explain away or even to defend social inequality. But an impatience with the ideal of equality is to be found even among those who identify with the contemporary centre left. For example, David Goodhart, editor of the crashingly dull British monthly *Prospect,* recently declared:

The old fixation with the 'gap' [between rich and poor] is the problem. A third way theory of fairness should state that the gap does not matter – or at least that it matters less than the life-chances of the people at the bottom. If these are rising steadily then it does not matter that the rich are getting even richer . . . 'Gap' thinking is also based on a defunct zero-sum idea of wealth creation. In a 19th-century mining village it was clear that the mine owner's wealth in a sense caused the poverty of the miners. Other than the odd sweat-shop, that is not the case today. The poverty of the poor does not create the richness of the rich and vice versa. Bill Gates has not amassed a fortune of $150 billion by exploiting the poor of Seattle.[27]

The evidence presented in the previous section should be sufficient to put in question Goodhart's complacent belief that 'the life-chances of the people at the bottom', or indeed of the majority, 'are rising steadily'. His remarks about Bill Gates are indicative of the reverential attitude that supporters of the Third Way adopt towards the super-rich. This represents something of a cultural shift certainly on the British left, if one recalls Denis Healey's promise in 1973, when unveiling to a delighted Labour Party conference the tax changes that he implemented after becoming Labour Chancellor of the Exchequer the following year: 'There are going to be howls of anguish from the eighty thousand people who are rich enough to pay over seventy five per cent on the last slice of their income.'[28] By contrast, in a recent joint policy statement Tony Blair and Gerhard Schröder announced: 'we want a society which celebrates successful entrepreneurs just as it does artists and footballers'.[29] Whether this ambition is consistent with the egalitarian professions both leaders also make is something we will explore in the rest of this book.

In any case, the ideal of equality is too deeply embedded in the political culture of the Western liberal democracies to be simply dismissed as 'defunct'. In a striking and widely discussed essay, the Italian political philosopher Norberto Bobbio recently challenged the idea that the collapse of the Communist bloc had rendered the distinction between left and right obsolete. Drawing on both historical and conceptual considerations, he argued that 'the criterion most frequently used to distinguish between the left and the right is the attitude of real people in society to the ideal of equality'. Pointing to the facts of global inequality, Bobbio declared:

> Faced with this reality there is a very clear distinction between the right and the left, for which the ideal of equality has always been the pole star that guides it. One only has to shift one's attention from the social questions within individual states which gave rise to socialism in the last century to the international social question in order to realize that the left has not only not completed its task, it has hardly commenced it.[30]

Bobbio seems to me fundamentally right.[31] If the left is not committed to equality, then it cannot be said to exist in any meaningful sense. But neither the existence nor the nature of this commitment can be taken for granted. Goodhart's clumsy attack on 'gap thinking' did at least have the merit of drawing attention to the confusion in contemporary thinking about equality. Rarely has this confusion been better exemplified than in Tony Blair's announcement: 'The class war is over. But the struggle for true equality has just begun.'[32]

This little book is intended to reinforce Bobbio's argument in three ways. In the first place, in the following chapter, I consider the historical meaning of the modern ideal of equality, tracing its origins in the great bourgeois revolutions of the seventeenth and eighteenth centuries and its development in socialist thought. Secondly, it is a remarkable fact that, in the past generation, while social and economic inequalities have been growing dramatically, the English-speaking world has produced a group of philosophers committed, despite their other differences, to articulating a rigorous and defensible egalitarian conception of social justice. Their founding text is, of course, John Rawls's great book *A Theory of Justice*, first published in 1971, but, among others, Ronald Dworkin, Amartya Sen, T.M. Scanlon, G.A. Cohen, Brian Barry, Thomas Nagel, Richard Arneson and John Roemer have contributed to an extraordinarily rich and sophisticated debate.

Probably the best description of this philosophical current is 'egalitarian liberalism'.[33] 'Liberalism' is understood here in the North American sense: like social democrats, egalitarian liberals favour state intervention in and regulation of the market (but not its abolition) in the interests of social justice. The subtlety and depth of these philosophers' efforts to clarify and defend the concept of equality have been in more or less inverse proportion to their influence on public policy.[34] One aim of this book is bring their work to bear on current political debates: this I seek to do in chapter 3, which is devoted to a discussion of some of the leading themes of egalitarian liberalism. Thirdly, in the concluding chapter I return to the state of the contemporary world, considering some of the causal connections between the inequalities documented above and the economic structures of capitalism: understanding these connections, as I try to show, is a necessary condition of devising any political strategy capable of translating the philosophical theory of egalitarian justice into reality.

Jacques Bidet has recently lamented the 'schizophrenia' in which

> contemporary critical thought seems to oscillate between a recourse to the sociologies of suspicion to which Marx opened the way, when it wants to think the world as it is, and a fascination with contractualism, with the doctrine of the rule of law [*l'Etat de droit*], the rights of man and of the citizen, when it is trying to formulate a social project [*un projet de société*].[35]

I would not for a moment claim to have overcome here this schizophrenia between Marx and Rawls, between critical social theory and normative political philosophy. Nevertheless, it does seem to me essential when considering the question of equality and inequality to engage in both – that is, to offer both philosophical arguments and socio-economic analysis. Arguably, this requirement is a crucial feature of *A Theory of Justice* itself. Brian Barry writes:

> If Rawls had achieved nothing else, he would have been important for having taken seriously the idea that the subject of justice is what he calls 'the basic structure of society' . . . Where we talk about the basic structure of society we are concerned with the way in which institutions work systematically so as to advantage some and disadvantage others. Rawls's incorporation of this idea of a social structure into his theory represents the coming of age of liberal political philosophy. For the first time, a major figure in the broadly individualistic tradition has taken account of the legacy of Marx and Weber by recognizing explicitly that societies have patterns of inequality that persist over time and systematic ways of allocating people to positions within their hierarchies of power, status and money.[36]

This implication of Rawls's theoretical enterprise has not, however, been much reflected in the intellectual practice of either political philosophers or social theorists – hence the oscillation of which Bidet complains. In this book, however, I seek to engage with both philosophical concepts and socio-economic structures. In doing so, I concentrate to a large extent on Britain, and therefore inevitably touch on the debates provoked by the New Labour 'project'. This may seem to involve the error, wittily denounced by Gore Vidal during the 1997 general election, of paying excessive attention to the affairs of a mere province of the American empire. Nevertheless, Britain under New Labour has come to play a certain exemplary role. It is true that the basic idea of the Third Way as a strategy for the 'centre left' (an expression whose popularity is itself a sign of the influence of American 'New Democrats', for whom the word 'socialism' is unmentionable) was coined by Bill Clinton and his advisors in the run-up to the 1992 presidential election. The contemporary United States is frequently cited as a model by New Labour.

But, after a White House seminar devoted to the Third Way drew, along with Clinton and Blair, the German Chancellor, and the prime ministers of Italy and the Netherlands, one of New Labour's most assiduous media courtiers announced that 'the Third Way project . . . is extraordinarily successful. It began as a British-American ideological venture; now European and other leaders are turning to it for inspiration, because they think it may have something that helps them to understand a shifting, shrinking world.'[37] There may be some virtue, then, in considering the egalitarian claims of the Third Way where it is pursued with all the formidable powers of a British government with a large parliamentary majority. '*De te fabula narratur!*' – 'the story is told of you', to quote Marx's warning to the world that it too would suffer the travails of industrial capitalism first experienced by Britain.[38]

Finally, I should perhaps say a word about the position from which this book is written. My own intellectual and political starting point is the classical Marxist tradition. For reasons that I touch in chapters 2 and 3, Marx and his successors were at best ambivalent about equality conceived as an ethical ideal. One of the attractions of egalitarian liberalism is that it offers intellectual resources with which to help remedy the resulting gaps in the Marxist tradition.[39] Nevertheless, this book is emphatically *not* an attempt to develop a Marxist theory of egalitarian justice. Rather, my concern is to consider the best contemporary philosophical work on equality, and to show that taking its political implications seriously would require a dramatic transformation of the present social and economic order. If there is anything distinctively Marxist about this book, it lies in the contradiction it seeks to expose between the normative claims of egalitarian liberalism, which does not directly challenge capitalist institutions, and the continued existence of these institutions.[40]

2

Equality and the Revolution

The dynamic of modernity

As a concrete social and political demand, equality is a child of the great revolutions that inaugurated the modern world. 'The poorest he that is in England has a life to live as the richest he, and therefore . . . every man that is to live under a government ought first by his own consent to put himself under that government,' said Colonel Rainborough, a leader of the Levellers, the radical wing of the English Revolution, during the Putney debates of October 1647.[1] 'We hold these truths to be self-evident: that all men are created equal; that they are endowed by their creator with certain inalienable rights; that among these are life, liberty, & the pursuit of happiness . . .' Nearly fifty years after he wrote these words in the American Declaration of Independence of 1776, Thomas Jefferson reaffirmed the same view in his very last letter: 'The general spread of the light of science has already laid open to every view the palpable truth, that the mass of mankind has not been born with saddles on their backs, nor a favoured few booted and spurred, ready to ride them legitimately, by the grace of God.'[2] And, of course, the Great French Revolution of 1789–94 nailed to its mast the watch-words *liberté, égalité, fraternité*.

Equality as a political ideal thus emerged from the struggle against the hierarchical order of the European *ancien régime*: even the American revolutionaries of 1776 turned against the Hanoverian state the ideologies of republican liberty and natural rights that had played their part in the seventeenth-century battles against Stuart absolutism. To a society where an ordered structure of ranks and estates was supposed to reflect the divine will was counterposed one where all had a right to consent to and participate in their government. As such, then, equality was conceived essentially as a *political* condition, justifying, as Rainborough argues, government by consent rather than any changes to the social and economic structure. Indeed, the fear of the propertied classes that enfranchising the propertyless masses would lead to social revolution ensured that even manhood suffrage made only fitful progress in Europe during the century after the French Revolution.

Nevertheless, comparatively early on in this protracted process, Alexis de Tocqueville in *Democracy in America* (1835, 1840) discerned the emergence of a new form of society characterized by 'equality of condition'. Tocqueville's analysis of democratic society conceived equality less as a well-defined normative concept, or a specific set of institutions or social structures, than as a *mentalité* or structure of feeling. 'Equality of condition' represented the absence of the status hierarchy constitutive of aristocratic societies and therefore was consistent with the existence of considerable differences in wealth and income. Tocqueville was chiefly interested in tracing the spiritual consequences of this new social order, its effects on how citizens conceived themselves and their relationship to public life; in doing so, he formulated a remarkably prescient account of the privatized individualism that is so central a feature of modern Western societies.[3]

It is, however, the failure to realize equality as an ideal, rather than these supposed consequences of 'equality of condition', that has dominated the modern debate. The contrast between aspiration and reality is built into the initial formulations of the ideal. Most obviously, Rainborough and Jefferson speak of the equality of *men*. The Levellers sought actually to enfranchise only property-owners. Jefferson, notoriously, was a Virginia slave-owner: 'how is it that we hear the loudest *yelps* for liberty from the drivers of negroes?' asked Dr Johnson during the American Revolution.[4] The ideal of equality came, it seemed, packed with tacit or explicit clauses excluding women, the poor, slaves and many other groups from its ambit.

In a remarkable essay, Etienne Balibar has suggested that these limitations imply not the abandonment of equality as an ideal, but its radicalization. He argues that the fundamental meaning of the main programmatic document of the French Revolution, the Declaration of the Rights of Man and of the Citizen of August 1789, is precisely the equation of Man and Citizen: individual humans, simply by virtue of their humanity, are political subjects. This equation, however, implies another, that of equality and liberty. This is what Balibar calls '*the proposition of égaliberté*'. By this 'deliberately baroque . . . portmanteau-word' he does not mean 'the intuitive discovery or the revelation of an identity of the *ideas* of Equality and of Liberty'. Rather, 'it is the historical discovery, which one could in fact call experimental, that their *extensions* are necessarily identical. To put it plainly, that the *situations* in which each is present or absent are necessarily the same.' In other words: '*There are no examples* of restrictions or suppression of liberties without social inequalities, nor of inequalities without restriction or suppression of liberties.'[5]

Balibar draws two main implications from the idea of
égaliberté:

> the meaning of the equation Man = Citizen is not so much
> the definition of a political right as the affirmation *of a
> universal right to politics*. Formally at least – but this is the
> very type of a form that can become a material weapon –
> the Declaration opens up an indefinite sphere of the 'polit-
> icization' of demands for rights which reiterate, each in its
> own way, the requirement of a citizenship or of an institu-
> tional, public, inscription of liberty and equality: in this
> indefinite opening is inscribed as well – and as early as the
> period of the Revolution one sees the attempt – the
> demand for the right of wage-earners or dependants such
> as women and slaves, later that of the colonized. This right
> finds itself formulated later in the following form: *the
> emancipation of the oppressed can only be their own work*,
> which underlines its ethical significance.[6]

Balibar argues, secondly, that intrinsic to 'the proposition
of *égaliberté*' is its 'absolute *indeterminacy*'. There is always
a discrepancy between the abstract equation of equality
and liberty and the concrete historical circumstances in
which a particular version of this statement is uttered:
'*There will be a permanent tension* between the conditions
that historically determine the construction of institutions
conforming to the proposition of *égaliberté*, and the hyper-
bolic universality of the statement.'[7] This tension gives the
idea an inherently subversive character.

   This account of *égaliberté* runs contrary to one of the
main assumptions of the liberal tradition, which, from
Tocqueville and John Stuart Mill to John Rawls and Isaiah
Berlin, has tended to treat equality and freedom as necessarily in conflict with one another. I return briefly to this
issue in chapter 3 below. For the present, it is more
important to stress that Balibar offers an intriguing analy-

sis of how the political demands of the great revolutions
of the seventeenth and eighteenth centuries have an inherent tendency to outflank themselves. Ideals that were
intended initially to have quite a narrow reference, to
benefit primarily white men of property, proved capable
of indefinite extension. The result is a process of permanent revolution in which a succession of new political
subjects – workers, slaves, women, colonial subjects, people of colour, oppressed nationalities, lesbians and gays,
disabled people . . . – emerge to stake their claim to the
liberty and equality won by earlier struggles.

Jacques Bidet has constructed an ambitious theory
intended to show that this dynamic is inherent in modernity itself. He argues that all modern societies presuppose
what he calls a 'metastructure' constituted above all by
'contractuality', which embraces both the transactions
among individuals on the market and the social contract
by which autonomous agents agree to govern themselves.
The aspiration to *égaliberté* implicit in this metastructure
is, however, 'reversed' in the structures of domination and
exploitation that survived the *ancien régime*. But, Bidet
insists, 'in modernity, domination, exploitation and vio-
lence are based on a, metastructural, reference to contractuality, to free and equal relations'. Thus, for example,
the structure of class inequality 'cannot be conceived
except by starting from it [the metastructure], as its
"reversal": the structure constitutes itself (and therefore
can only conceive itself) in the reversal of the principle it
poses, it builds itself under the form of the promise
unfulfilled, the pact denied'.[8]

Bidet's concept of the metastructure doesn't seem to
me particularly helpful inasmuch as it rests on the claim
that modern societies are best understood by starting from
the promise of *égaliberté* that constantly shadows their
progress. As Bidet himself says, 'the metastructure only

ever advances in the conditions of the structure, in conflict'.[9] In other words, the demand for freedom and equality is made in societies that systematically deny it, that indeed are riven by social and political struggles. What is it about the structure of these societies that encourages the aspiration towards *égaliberté*? In my view, it is the contrast between the fact that capitalist societies treat their members as legally free and equal and the systematic socio-economic inequalities that they still harbour in their depths. Thus Marx argues that 'the concept of human equality' can acquire 'the permanence of a fixed popular opinion ... only in a society where ... the dominant social relation is the relation between men as possessors of commodities' – a relationship that, as we shall shortly see, he believes gives rise to capitalist exploitation.[10] This structural conflict feeds the political discourse of freedom and equality rather than, as Bidet suggests, that discourse providing the necessary starting-point for understanding modernity.[11]

In any case, however precisely we theoretically interpret it, the historical reality seems plain enough. Since the Enlightenment and the French Revolution, no inherited institution or practice can any longer claim justification by appeal to tradition or to divine sanction. Every social relationship is open to question, in an endless debate in which every human must be treated as an autonomous subject possessing the same rights as others. The rectification of particular injustices – for example, the status hierarchy of the old regime or New World chattel slavery – simply draws attention to others – the exploitation of workers, say, or the racial oppression of black people – that themselves demand remedy. The very generality of the demand for *égaliberté* puts it in permanent conflict with the particular historical conditions that prevail at any time.

This analysis casts Tocqueville's account of 'equality of

condition' in a different light. It suggests a more dynamic picture, in which existing social and political arrangements are constantly liable to subversion by new demands to extend the application of *égaliberté*. If this is right, then the proposals cited in the previous chapter that we abandon the search for equality are likely to be disappointed: as long as there are significant discrepancies in wealth and power, there will be movements denouncing them as unjustified and demanding their removal.

Socialism and equality:
Marx, Tawney, Crosland

The significance of socialism in this context is that it originated in the recognition of the discrepancy between the French Revolution's promise of *égalité* and the reality of the society that emerged from the upheavals after 1789. Theodore Zeldin describes the concrete form taken by this discrepancy in the Napoleonic Code Civil:

> Troplong, First President of the Cour de Cassation, and author of the leading commentary on the Civil Code . . ., revealingly declared himself satisfied with it because he considered that democracy existed when men have an equal right to the protection of the law 'in conditions of inequality which they have created for themselves by the legitimate exercise of their natural powers'. The Civil Code certainly confirmed these inequalities. It had a narrow view of citizenship, which it confused with the possession of property, and so it made the penniless worker almost an outlaw. It was concerned not with making men equal but with protecting property.[12]

This duplicitous equality is well captured by Anatole France's *bon mot*: 'The bourgeois law forbids with the same majesty both the rich and the poor to sleep under the bridge.' But it was Marx who subjected it to the most stringent analysis. In a famous passage in *Capital*, he considers the contract struck by capitalist and worker on the labour market. This transaction takes place in the 'sphere of circulation or commodity-exchange',

> a very Eden of the innate rights of man. It is the exclusive realm of Freedom, Equality, Property, and Bentham. Freedom, because both buyer and seller of a commodity, let us say labour-power, are determined only by their own free will. They contract as free persons, who are equal before the law . . . Equality, because each enters into the relation with the other, as with a simple owner of commodities, and they exchange equivalent for equivalent. Property, because each disposes only of what is his own. And Bentham, because each looks to his own advantage.[13]

Once, however, we follow the capitalist and the worker into 'the hidden abode of production', the picture changes. The equality between them is only formal; really they are unequal. For the worker is 'free in the double sense that as a free individual he can dispose of his labour-power as his own commodity, and that, on the other hand, he has no other commodity for sale, i.e. he is rid of them, he is free of all the objects needed for the realization [*Verwirklichung*] of his labour'. The worker enjoys political and legal freedom: he does not suffer from the kind of personal disabilities imposed on slaves or serfs. At the same time, however, his only economically relevant property is his labour-power. Denied access to the means of production, he is 'compelled by social conditions to sell the whole of his active life, his capacity for labour'.[14] The capitalist uses his control of the means of production to strike a highly favourable bargain: once employed, the worker produces commodities for the capitalist under the latter's control in exchange for a wage that represents only part of the value he creates. The worker's apparent freedom and equality with the capitalist conceal an underlying subordination and inequality whose outcome is the former's exploitation.

Marx's account of capitalist exploitation, and in particular the burning anger with which he describes the condition of the working class, naturally invites the response that he is morally condemning capitalism for violating some universal principle of justice. The ostensibly egalitarian 'needs principle' that he puts forward in the 'Critique of the Gotha Programme' – 'From each according to his abilities, to each according to his needs!' – could be taken as the basis of his theory of justice.[15] Yet Marx is consistently hostile to any appeal to normative concepts. Underlying this stance seems to be the belief that the materialist conception of history entails a relativist account of ethics in which moral discourse is reduced to a reflection of the requirements of the prevailing mode of production. This implies that there are no universal ethical principles applicable to all forms of society. Yet Marx himself describes capitalist exploitation as the '*theft of alien labour-time*', which, since he also makes it clear that this exploitation does not violate capitalist property laws, implies appeal to some transhistorical principle of justice.[16]

Norman Geras, in his definitive treatment of this highly controversial subject, offers the following proposal for making sense of Marx's contradictory statements on justice and exploitation: 'Marx did think capitalism was unjust but he did not think he thought so.'[17] In other words, Marx's erroneous meta-ethical theory prevented him from seeing universal moral principles as anything but the expression of historically specific class interests and therefore from recognizing the basis on which he himself condemned capitalist exploitation. This confusion does not, however, stop Marx highlighting in the 'Critique of the Gotha Programme' an important problem concerning the relationship between any principle of egalitarian justice and individual differences, but, as I argue when discussing this problem in chapter 3, he is best understood here as proposing a more complex egalitarianism rather than as rejecting it altogether.

Marx also had a more directly political objection to basing socialist demands on appeal to some principle of distributive justice, namely that it limits these demands to the partial reform rather than revolutionary transformation of capitalism. Thus he argued that proposals for redistribution tended to focus on the redistribution of income, reflecting a failure to recognize that '[a]ny distribution whatever of the means of consumption is only a consequence of the distribution of the conditions of production themselves.'[18] Workers' exclusion from the means of production was responsible for their exploitation. Only a revolution through which they gained control of these resources offered a real remedy: the redistribution of income through, for example, wage increases and progressive taxation offered only the partial, and necessarily fragile, amelioration of a fundamentally exploitive condition.

On the face of it, however, there seems no logically compelling reason why a concern with distribution should necessarily confine itself to that of the means of consumption rather than that of the means of production. Indeed, in the following passage from *Capital*, Marx himself seems to treat the collective ownership of the most basic productive resource – the land – as a moral principle:

From the standpoint of a higher socio-economic formation, the private property of particular individuals in the earth will appear just as absurd as the private property of one man in other men. Even an entire society, a nation, or all

simultaneously existing societies taken together, are not the
owners of the earth. They are simply its possessors, its
beneficiaries, and have to bequeath it in an improved state
to succeeding generations, as *boni patres familias* [good
householders].[19]

It is nevertheless true, as we shall see in the two subsequent chapters, that egalitarian theorists often focus on
the redistribution of income rather than that of productive
assets. This is generally the case, for example, with the
social-democratic tradition, where the problem of equality
has attracted far more attention than among Marxists.
Among the Fabians, for example, Shaw advocated equality of income: 'the only satisfactory plan is to give everybody an equal share no matter what sort of person she is,
or how old she is, or what sort of work she does, or who
or what her father was'.[20]

Equality also stands at the centre of the thought of two
of the most influential figures in the British Labourist
tradition, R.H. Tawney and Anthony Crosland. Tawney,
writing during the Great Depression of the 1930s, did not
rely on any claim that humans are equal in capacity or
attainment – indeed, in a passage that offers a salutary
warning of the historical relativity of apparently solid
scientific judgements, he appealed to 'Dr Burt's admirable
studies of the distribution of educational abilities among
school-children', studies which have long since been
exposed as resting on the fraudulent manipulation of the
evidence from IQ tests.[21]

Even the economic inequality that Tawney documented
was of concern primarily for its moral and spiritual consequences: 'the machinery of existence – property and
material wealth and industrial organization, and the whole
fabric and mechanism of social institutions – is to be
regarded as a means to an end, and . . . this end is the

growth towards perfection of individual human beings'. The chief evil of the class divisions in mid-twentieth-century Britain lay in the tendency they implied to value individuals according to their wealth and income. Equality of opportunity in a society where the concentration of economic power placed individuals in very different circumstances was insufficient to remedy this situation: 'In the absence of a large measure of equality of circumstances, opportunities to rise must necessarily be illusory. Given such equality, opportunities to rise will look after themselves.' The restoration of moral community depended on the reduction of inequalities in economic power and in 'inequality of circumstance or condition, such as arises when some social groups are deprived of the necessaries of civilization which others enjoy'.[22]

The remedy to this situation lay, Tawney believed, less in redistribution as such than in a reordering of social and political priorities: 'What is important is not that all men should receive the same pecuniary income. It is that the surplus resources of society should be husbanded and applied so that it is a matter of minor significance whether they receive it or not.' Achieving this shift in priorities required the expansion of social provision financed by progressive taxation; the restriction of capitalist power by trade-union action and legislation; and the extension of publicly or co-operatively owned enterprises. It is fair to say that public ownership occupies a privileged place in the policies advocated by Tawney. This reflected both his principled belief that what he regarded as essential industries should be in public hands for reasons of democracy and efficiency, and a strategic judgement that nationalization was necessary to overcome capitalist opposition:

All attacks on inequality, whatever the method employed, encounter determined resistance from the privileged classes, during recent years, that resistance has hardened. It is an illusion to suppose that either of the first two policies [i.e. expanded welfare provision and trade-union action] can be carried forward on the scale, or with the speed required, as long as the key positions of the economic system remain in private hands.[23]

Crosland, by contrast, famously sought to reduce the profile of nationalization in social-democratic strategy. Writing as the Long Boom of the 1950s and 1960s began to gather pace, he argued that the combined effect of structural changes in capitalism – in particular, the concentration of economic power in the hands of large corporations whose objectives were much more complex than the maximization of short-term profit – and the new power of governments to achieve full employment thanks to Keynesian techniques of demand-management had made the private ownership of the means of production a non-issue. Nevertheless, Crosland insisted (in a manner that in some respects anticipates Bobbio's recent arguments) that there was still a fundamental difference between left and right, arising from the socialist commitment to equality:

> The socialist seeks a distribution of rewards, status, and privileges egalitarian enough to minimize social resentment, to secure justice between individuals, and to equalize opportunities; and he seeks to weaken the deep-seated class stratification, with its concomitant feelings of envy and inferiority, and the barriers to inhibited mingling among the classes. This belief in social equality, which has been the strongest ethical inspiration of virtually every socialist doctrine, still remains the most characteristic feature of socialist thought today.[24]

Crosland offered three arguments for increasing social equality. Two were instrumental, namely that 'greater

equality . . . will increase social contentment and diminish
social resentment' and that 'extreme social inequality . . .
is wasteful and inefficient'. The third was more principled,
since it 'rests on a view of what constitutes a "just"
distribution of privileges and rewards'. Under this heading, Crosland advanced a heterogeneous collection of
considerations. Three in particular stand out. First, 'every
child' has 'a natural "right", not merely to "life, liberty,
and the pursuit of happiness", but to the position in the
social scale to which his native talents entitle him: he
should have, in other words, an equal opportunity for
wealth, advancement, and renown'. This right was vio-
lated by the existence of private education and inherited
wealth. Secondly, '[t]he greater the inequality, the heavier
the concentration of power.' Thirdly, while inequality of
incomes from work was acceptable, 'both because
superior talent deserves some rent of ability, and because
otherwise certain kinds of work, or risk, or burdensome
responsibility will not be shouldered', 'it is not clear that
these considerations justify the present pattern of work-
rewards'.[25]

The differences between Crosland and Tawney are
obvious. Not simply did they place a different emphasis
on the role of public ownership in reducing inequality, but
Crosland's hedonist individualism – reflected in his
famous attack on the Puritanism of the Webbs and his
call for 'a greater emphasis on private life, on freedom and
dissent, culture, beauty, leisure, and even frivolity' – sat ill
with Tawney's Christian-socialist preoccupation with
moral community.[26] Yet there are also striking similarities
between their views on equality. Both, for example, shared
a fierce hatred of Britain's so-called public schools: 'The
idea that differences of educational opportunity among
children should depend upon differences of wealth among
parents is a barbarity,' Tawney wrote.[27] This reflected a

shared belief that more democratic access to education represented a critical means of reducing inequalities: as Education Secretary in 1965–7, Crosland took the decisive step in introducing comprehensive education in state schools.[28]

But, beyond these more specific concerns lay a common belief that, to put it crudely, history was going their way. Both Tawney and Crosland thought that the growth of what Rudolph Hilferding called 'organized capitalism' – national economies dominated by large corporations interwoven with the state – radically transformed the prospects for democratic control over the economy. Social-democratic parties needed only to develop the political will and vision to make that control a reality and use it to reduce social inequality. Of the two, Crosland more closely fitted Marx's view that reformist socialists are concerned with the redistribution of income rather than with that of productive resources. Yet, even judged by the policy agenda that he sought to set, the Labour governments in which he served in the 1960s and 1970s took hardly any steps towards greater equality. Indeed, the 1974–9 government of Harold Wilson and James Callaghan saw the beginnings of the trend towards a wider gap between rich and poor discussed in chapter 1.

This is part of a wider set of economic and social changes among whose chief features are: a secular fall in the rate of growth in the advanced economies compared to the 'Golden Age' after the Second World War; the decline of 'organized capitalism' as even the most powerful nation-states have found it increasingly difficult to control economic life within their own borders; and, concomitantly, the internationalization of capital, reflected most visibly in the spectacular increase in both the quantity and the mobility of capital invested in globally integrated financial markets. More than anything else it is these changes that, it is argued, make the traditional socialist agenda represented in their different ways by Marx, Tawney and Crosland obsolete, and require the reinvention of social democracy along the lines of the Third Way advocated by Tony Blair and Bill Clinton. In the following chapters, I seek first to clarify the meaning of equality as a normative concept, before considering the conditions of its realization in the contemporary world.

3

Equality and the Philosophers

New Labour and socialist values

New Labour presents itself as the heir of the social-democratic tradition. It seeks a Third Way between traditional 'state socialism' and the neo-liberalism of the Reagan–Thatcher era, but one based on traditional socialist values. Thus Gordon Brown, the most ideologically self-conscious New Labour leader, is careful to seek to situate himself with respect to Crosland's legacy, both stressing the economic changes since the 1950s – globalization, chronic mass unemployment and so on – and insisting that, 'far from marginalizing the issue of equality, these changes mean the case for equality is even stronger'.[1] Crosland can indeed be regarded as the author of that standard New Labour topos 'Traditional Values in a Modern Setting'. He argued: 'The only constant element, common to all the bewildering variety of different [socialist] doctrines, consists of certain moral values and aspirations; and people have called themselves socialists because they shared these aspirations.' Accordingly, he attacked attempts to equate socialism with specific means, notably nationalization, aimed at realizing these values and aspirations.[2] Precisely this distinction between values and means was used to justify the deletion in 1995 of the commitment to public ownership from Clause Four of the Labour Party's constitution.

What then are these eternal socialist values? Here is a sample, from a joint policy document from Tony Blair and the German Chancellor, Gerhard Schröder: 'Fairness and social justice, liberty and equality of opportunity, solidarity and responsibility to others – these values are timeless. Social democracy will never sacrifice them. To make these values relevant to today's world requires realistic and forward-looking policies capable of meeting the challenges of the 21st century.'[3] On the basis of material of this kind, Alan Carling argues that 'the Third Way's values apparently boil down to: autonomy, community, democracy and equality'. He goes on to say that these are identical to 'the core values of socialism' that he had sought independently to define from 'an Analytical Marxist perspective'.[4] One might then say that socialists have traditionally argued that these values can be realized only where productive resources are subject to collective and democratic control.[5]

The values of autonomy, community, democracy and equality do indeed seem like a good starting-point for our discussion. In the first place, treating these as core values serves to indicate that egalitarians are not committed to equality to the exclusion of all other virtues. The inter-relations between these different ideals raise complex and important issues. It may be, for example, that realizing one may undermine another: such has been the classical liberal stance on the relationship between liberty and equality. It may also be that giving proper weight to community may limit the restrictions that can legitimately be placed on equality. (I return to both of these issues in the next section.) Secondly, the fact that New Labour's ethical commitments are apparently identical with those of more traditional socialists offers an opportunity to appraise the Third Way in terms that both its adherents and its left-wing critics would acknowledge as valid.[6]

Once, however, we move beyond affirmations of general principle, the ground becomes much boggier. Attempts by exponents of the Third Way to specify the nature of their commitment to equality are vague and sometimes ambiguous. There are two main variants of New Labour equality. One, chiefly identified with Gordon Brown, contrasts equality of outcome with equality of opportunity. The first, which he associates with Croslandite critics of New Labour such as Roy Hattersley, 'would not only leave the causes of poverty unaddressed but requires a prescribed, centralist imposition of outcomes, pays little regard to effort or desert and would threaten a state where opportunities are provided not imposed'. Brown prefers 'a maximalist equality of opportunity' that is 'recurrent, lifelong, and comprehensive: political, social and economic opportunities for all, with an obligation by Government to pursue them relentlessly'. Such equality is not merely enjoined by considerations of social justice: 'now in the 1990s in the new economy, equality of opportunity is also the key to economic prosperity. Why? Because we are in a fast-changing information-based economy dominated by the importance of knowledge, the skills of people and their ability to act.' Thus, a government that devotes resources to the education and training of disadvantaged individuals will find virtue rewarded, since a consequence will be enhanced economic competitiveness.[7]

A fawning profile credited Brown with 'elaborating . . . a political philosophy of vast scope', 'a theoretical edifice that challenges and is meant to challenge the main reference points of British socialism of the past century – from Marxism through Tawneyite egalitarianism to Croslandite revisionism'.[8] This seems, on the face of it, an excessively generous description. Equality of opportunity is in fact an ambiguous concept embracing at least three distinct kinds of equality. First of all, it can simply mean the formal prohibition of discrimination on the basis of attributes other than those strictly relevant to the position for which individuals concerned are being considered. The experience of the United States over the past generation, where the dismantling of legalized segregation as a result of the Civil Rights movement of the 1960s has not led to any significant overall improvement in the condition of most African-Americans, indicates that this version of equality of opportunity is compatible with the persistence of structural inequalities.[9]

Secondly, equality of opportunity can mean meritocracy, where the distribution of income reflects individual talent and effort. In such a society, rewards are unequally distributed, but competition to gain access to these rewards is open. One obvious difficulty arises from the interaction of equal starting-points with unequal destinations: one does not have to be too pessimistic about human nature to expect that the better off under such an arrangement would seek to ensure that their offspring started the race ahead of their subordinates' children. Thirdly, what Carling calls 'deep' equality of opportunity requires an extensive equalization of resources to ensure that the competition for positions is genuinely open: but so thorough-going is the required redistribution that this version of equality of opportunity bears little resemblance to the two others.[10]

Brown does reject what he calls 'narrow equality of opportunity', and even on occasion endorses Rawls's difference principle, declaring that 'wealth and incomes inequalities . . . can be justified only if they are in the interests of the least fortunate'.[11] I consider in chapter 4 how far Brown's policies match up to these highly demanding egalitarian principles.

The other main New Labour conceptualization of equality and inequality is in terms of, respectively, inclusion and exclusion. This is reflected at the level of policy in the attachment of a Social Exclusion Unit to the Cabinet Office at 10 Downing Street, but it also forms one of main themes of Anthony Giddens's book *The Third Way*. For Giddens:

> Two forms of exclusion are becoming marked in contemporary societies. One is the exclusion of those at the bottom, cut off from the mainstream of opportunities society has to offer. At the top is voluntary exclusion, 'the revolt of the elites': a withdrawal from public institutions on the part of more affluent groups, who choose to live separately from the rest of society.[12]

The phenomena to which Giddens refers undoubtedly exist. Yet his treatment of them is, to say the least, curious. For one thing, as Carling protests,

> [i]t is a pretty astonishing move . . . to *assimilate* the social positions of those at the very top and the very bottom of social structure to a single social category – the excluded – especially as this result occurs by such very different mechanisms: people who could easily join the mainstream, but choose not to do so are lumped together with those who lack the wherewithal for joining the mainstream however much they might wish.[13]

Furthermore, even if the assimilation were tenable, it seems unclear why the withdrawals of rich and poor should constitute an instance of *inequality*. It would seem rather to represent a breakdown in community, or, at most, a reason for reducing inequality because of its negative consequences for social cohesion. What is thus occluded in this discussion is any consideration of inequality as a problem of distributive justice. Indeed, Carling notes, Giddens ignores 'the extensive debate . . . on the character of social justice', and therefore his 'treatment of equality is extremely confused and uncertain'.[14] In a more recent discussion, Giddens combines question-begging attacks on 'the egalitarianism-at-all-costs that absorbed leftists for so long' with tendentious interpretation of the kind of studies of poverty and equality cited in chapter 1. These dubious arguments are used to support a 'dynamic conception of equality' that, in policy terms, seems to differ little from Brown's strategy.[15]

Giddens's lack of interest in principled discussion of equality and justice is by no means untypical of contemporary social democracy. G.A. Cohen protested bitterly at the way in which the Commission on Social Justice, appointed by the then Labour leader John Smith after the 1992 general election, 'bow[ed] down before the success of pro-market and anti-egalitarian ideology'.[16] The absence of any systematic analysis of equality in the literature of the Third Way suggests that there may be some political profit to be gained from considering the very rich philosophical discussions of the subject to be found in the writings of the egalitarian liberals. Brown himself has invoked the authority not merely of Rawls but of Amartya Sen and Michael Walzer, although without specifying in any very precise way the connection between their work and his own policies.[17] So what do the philosophers have to teach us about equality?

Rawls and the difference principle

John Rawls's monumental *A Theory of Justice* is a vast, labyrinthine, tortuously constructed book. Since its publication nearly thirty years ago – and alongside various essays intended by Rawls to elaborate on and sometimes to emend its theses, many themselves republished in revised form as *Political Liberalism* (1993) – the book has become the object of an enormous philosophical industry. I have no intention of contributing to this industry here. My focus is strictly on those aspects of the book that are directly relevant to the issue of equality.

A theory is often best understood by considering what it is written against. In Rawls's case it is utilitarianism. Over the past two centuries, utilitarianism has probably been the most influential intellectual tradition in the English-speaking world in the theoretical appraisal of public policy. It conceives the good as welfare-maximization: initially, welfare (or utility) was identified with pleasurable mental states, but in the more formal modern literature it tends to be treated as the satisfaction of a person's preferences for some states of affairs over others. Individuals are treated as rational choosers who, having ordered their preferences, seek to maximize their welfare as defined by these preferences. This conception of human agency informs the neo-classical orthodoxy in economics. As an ethical theory, utilitarianism judges actions by their consequences: we are to seek those outcomes that achieve the greatest sum of satisfactions for society at large. In Jeremy Bentham's words: 'An action then may be said to be conformable to the principle of utility . . . when the tendency it has to augment the happiness of the community is greater than any it has to diminish it.'[18]

There is an important sense in which utilitarianism, which was given its canonical formulation by Bentham in the era of the American and French Revolutions, is egalitarian in spirit, as is reflected by his axiom 'everybody to count for one, nobody for more than one'.[19] Nevertheless, the goal of welfare-maximization does not require an equal distribution of income or wealth. If, on some highly unequal distribution, the satisfaction of the rich so out-weighs the dissatisfaction of the poor that the sum of satisfied preferences is greater than that produced by any other, more egalitarian distribution, then utilitarians would have no reason to reject that state of affairs. Furthermore, utilitarianism may have highly illiberal consequences, since there may be cases where the general welfare of society could be increased at the expense of individual members of that society. As Rawls puts it, 'there is no reason in principle why the greater gains of some should not compensate for the lesser losses of some; or more importantly, why the violation of the liberty of a few might not be made right by the greater good shared by many.'[20]

For Rawls, this is a reflection of the fact that utilitarianism involves extending to society a model of individual choice: 'just as it is rational for one man to maximize the fulfilment of his system of desires, it is right for society to maximize the net balance of satisfaction taken over all its members'. This approach to social choice involves 'conflating all persons into one'. Thus: 'Utilitarianism does not take seriously the distinction between persons.'[21] Another way of making the same point is to say that utilitarianism violates Kant's third version of the Categorical Imperative: '*Act in such a way that you always treat humanity, whether in your own person or in the person of any other, never simply as a means, but always at the same time as an end.*'[22] If utilitarianism enjoins the non-fulfilment of my goals because this will contribute to a greater overall sum of satisfactions, then I am being treated only as a means and not as an end.

Liberal philosophers often invoke Kant's principle in order to ground individual rights. Robert Nozick, for example, argues that these rights should be conceived as 'side-constraints' that offer individuals moral protection against social action: 'they may not be sacrificed or used for the achieving of other ends without their consent . . . Side-constraints express the inviolability of other persons.'[23] Nozick proceeds to rule out redistribution according to some egalitarian 'end-state principle' because this would violate individual rights and thus the separateness of persons. What is remarkable about Rawls's philosophical strategy is that he too starts from a Kantian critique of utilitarianism, but nevertheless constructs on that basis an egalitarian theory of justice. In his scheme, as Brian Barry puts it, 'rights are a conclusion, not a premiss'.[24] Individual rights, in other words, are conceived not as primordial constraints on collective action, but as consequences of the requirements of a just social order.

Rawls proceeds by seeking to rehabilitate the social contract tradition of Locke, Rousseau and Kant. His principles of justice are those that would be chosen in a hypothetical 'original position'. The parties in the original position are conceived of as being rational actors in the rather narrow sense in which rationality is understood in the utilitarian tradition – that is, they order their preferences and seek the outcome that will maximize their welfare as defined by these preferences. But the parties must choose behind 'a veil of ignorance'. In particular,

> no one knows his place in society, his class position or social status; nor does he know his fortune in the distribution of natural assets and abilities, his intelligence and strength and the like. Nor, again, does anyone know his conception of the good, the particulars of his rational plan of life, or even the special features of his psychology such as his aversion to risk or liability to pessimism or optimism. More than this, I assume the parties do not know the particulars of their own society.[25]

The parties to the original position are furthermore confronted with what Hume called 'the circumstances of justice', which obtain 'whenever mutually disinterested persons put forward conflicting claims to the division of social advantages under conditions of moderate scarcity'.[26] The point of principles of distributive justice is to provide a mutually acceptable basis on which to regulate such conflicts. The subject of justice is what Rawls calls 'the basic structure of society',

> the way in which social institutions fit together into one system, and how they assign fundamental rights and duties and shape the division of advantage that arises through social co-operation. Thus the political constitution, the legally recognized forms of property, and the organization of the economy, and the nature of the family, all belong to the basic structure.[27]

Rawls argues that rational actors in the original position will choose two principles of justice. These concern the distribution of the 'primary social goods', that is, of

a. basic rights and liberties . . .;
b. freedom of movement and free choice of occupation against a background of diverse opportunities;
c. powers and prerogatives of offices and positions of responsibility in political and economic institutions of the basic structure;
d. income and wealth; and, finally,
e. the social bases of self-respect.[28]

What Rawls calls 'justice as fairness' involves the following:

First Principle
Each person is to have an equal right to the most extensive total system of equal basic liberties compatible with a similar system of liberty for all.

Second Principle
Social and economic inequalities are to be arranged so that
they are both:
(a) to the greatest benefit of the least advantaged, . . . and
(b) attached to offices and positions open to all under
     conditions of fair equality of opportunity.[29]

Not surprisingly, Rawls's derivation of these principles
has attracted much critical attention. Using the utilitarian
methods of rational-choice theory to arrive at liberal egalitarian conclusions is a remarkable intellectual feat, but
one that has provoked much scepticism. Even philosophers such as Barry who are sympathetic to Rawls's
basic enterprise argue that T.M. Scanlon's version of
contractarianism, which forbids those actions inconsistent
with principles that no one motivated to seek informed
and uncoerced general agreement could reasonably reject,
provides a better procedure for arriving at principles of
justice.[30]

Much more important for our purposes is the radically
egalitarian character of Rawls's second principle of justice,
the famous difference principle. Arguably this is the core
of his entire theory of justice. Indeed, he says 'the two
principles . . . are a special case of a more general conception of justice': 'All social values – liberty and opportunity,
income and wealth, and the bases of self-respect – are to
be distributed equally unless an unequal distribution of
any, or all, of these goods is to the advantage of the least
favoured.'[31] In other words, the presumption is in favour
of equality. Inequalities require justification by the benefits
they bring the least advantaged.

There is a further aspect of Rawls's radicalism. On one
interpretation of equality of opportunity, namely meritocracy, rewards are distributed according to individuals'
natural talents and the use they make of them. But, Rawls

argues, 'the initial endowment of natural assets and the
contingencies of their growth and nurture in early life are
arbitrary from a moral point of view'. The veil of ignorance conceals from the parties to the original position how
they have done in this distribution. Accordingly,

> the difference principle represents, in effect, an agreement
> to regard the distribution of natural talents as a common
> asset and to share in the benefits of this distribution
> whatever it turns out to be. Those who have been favoured
> by nature, whoever they are, may gain from their good
> fortune only on terms that improve the situation of those
> who have lost out. The naturally advantaged are not to
> gain merely because they are more gifted, but only to cover
> the costs of training and education and for using their
> endowments in ways that help the least fortunate as well.
> No one deserves his greater natural capacity nor merits a
> more favourable starting point in society. But it does not
> follow that one should eliminate these distinctions. There
> is another way to deal with them. The basic structure can
> be arranged so that these contingencies work for the benefit
> of the least fortunate. Thus we are led to the difference
> principle if we wish to set up the social system so that no
> one gains or loses from his arbitrary place in the distribu-
> tion of natural assets or his initial position in society
> without giving or receiving compensating advantages in
> return.[32]

Rawls thus throws into the pot, to be distributed
according to the principles of justice, not merely alienable
resources such as the means of production, but also the
benefits obtained from the use of the inalienable assets
inherent in individuals. No wonder this aspect of Rawls's
argument has been strenuously attacked by New Right
theorists such as Nozick, who insists that Kant's principle
of treating humans as ends requires that individuals are
entitled to their natural talents and to whatever they gain

through using them.[33] The difference principle thus
involves a deeper form of equality than equality of opportunity, at least as the latter concept is normally
understood.

Like many revolutionary works, *A Theory of Justice* is
deeply embedded in the tradition from which it emerged
– in this case, classical liberalism. This can be seen in two
respects in particular. First, there is what Rawls calls 'the
priority of liberty': that is, 'the precedence of the principle
of equal liberty over the second principle of justice. The
two principles of justice are in lexical order, and therefore
the claims of liberty are to be satisfied first . . . liberty can
be restricted only for the sake of liberty itself.'[34] Rawls's
arguments for this position are characteristically complex,
but they do not conceal the fact that he here reproduces
the traditional liberal belief in a conflict between individual freedom and social equality, and opts for the former.
He must then confront the historical claim, implicit in
Balibar's 'proposition of *égaliberté*', that attacks on liberties
are accompanied by increased inequalities, and vice versa
(see chapter 2). The privileged defend their position by
restricting individual freedoms, while such restrictions in
turn are likely to become the basis of new privileges.

Elsewhere in his system Rawls effectively acknowledges
that the relationship between liberty and equality is more
complex than is implied by the lexical priority he gives to
the first principle of justice over the second. A just consti-
tutional order must secure what he calls 'the fair value for
all political liberties': in other words, 'those similarly
endowed and motivated should have roughly the same
chance for attaining positions of political authority irres-
pective of their economic and social class'. But, in actually
existing liberal democracies, Rawls notes, '[d]isparities in
the distribution of property and wealth that far exceed
what is compatible with political equality have generally

been tolerated by the legal system.'[35] This is, of course, precisely the point that Marxists have always made when, as Rosa Luxemburg put it, they point to 'the hard core of social inequality and lack of freedom hidden under the sweet shell of formal equality and freedom'.[36] Indeed, in a recent text Rawls acknowledges that 'Hegel, Marxist, and socialist writers have been quite right in making this objection.' He goes on to specify the following institutional conditions for securing the fair value of liberties:

a. Public financing of elections and ways of assuring the availability of public information on matters of public policy . . .
b. A certain fair equality of opportunity, especially in education and training . . .
c. A decent distribution of wealth and income meeting the third condition of liberalism: all citizens must be assured of the all-purpose means necessary for them to take intelligent and effective advantage of their basic freedoms . . .
d. Society as employer of last resort through general or local government, or other social and economic policies . . .
e. Basic health care assured all citizens.[37]

So it turns out that giving effect to the first principle of justice depends on achieving a significant degree of socioeconomic equality. This surely supports Balibar's claim that liberty and equality go together, rather than – as the classical liberal tradition contends – necessarily being in conflict with one another. On effectively the same grounds, Jacques Bidet prefers Rawls's 'general conception' of justice to the two lexically ordered principles: 'Adequately understood, the generic principle of justice . . . stipulates that no difference with respect to liberty is acceptable, because no inequality of liberty can be to the advantage (whatever this might be) of those who have least.'[38]

The second respect in which Rawls's theory of justice is evidently deeply embedded in the classical liberal tradition is its background presumption of a market economy. For example, when considering different interpretations of the second principle of justice, he assumes that 'the economy is a free market system, although the means of production may or may not be privately owned'.[39] As Bidet notes, '[t]he disjunction between the two principles makes body with a division of the basic structure into two spheres, one politics, to which the first [principle] applies, the other economics, to which the second applies.' With respect to the latter, while in principle Rawls leaves open the choice between private or social ownership of the means of production, in effect 'he shows complete faith in the market economy to assure economic rationality and dynamism'.[40] Thus he considers the case of a 'property-owning democracy' where entrepreneurs enjoy much better prospects than unskilled labourers. This inequality can be justified under the difference principle if

> the greater expectations allowed to entrepreneurs encourages them to do things that raise the long-term prospects of labouring class [*sic*]. Their better prospects act as incentives so that the economic process is more efficient, innovation proceeds, and so on. Eventually the resulting material benefits spread throughout the system and to the least advantaged.[41]

Rawls stresses that this is a hypothetical example, but it is symptomatic of his thinking about incentives. We saw above that he believes that the difference principle justifies giving the talented extra rewards if this will encourage them to produce more and thereby to benefit the least advantaged. This claim has been subjected to detailed criticism by G.A. Cohen, who argues that it is inconsistent with better and worst off belonging to the same moral community (or, more precisely, what Cohen calls 'justificatory community'). The better off's claim to incentives is, in effect, a form of blackmail, in which they threaten not to make their contribution unless they are specially rewarded. This is a demand that is often made in situations of conflict, but, Cohen contends, it is not one that can be coherently made by one member of a justificatory community to another: members of such a community undertake to justify their actions to each other, and making a threat is not offering the kind of reason that could be accepted as a justification.[42] In the course of this critique, Cohen expresses his

> doubt that the difference principle justifies *any* significant inequality in an unqualified way . . . The worst off benefit from incentive inequality in particular only because the better off would, in effect, go on strike if unequalizing incentives were withdrawn. This inequality benefits the badly off within the constraint set by the inegalitarian attitude, and consequent behaviour, of the well off, a constraint that they could remove. And an inequality can also benefit the badly off within a constraint set, not by inegalitarian attitudes per se, but by preexisting unequal structures . . . I conjecture that social inequalities will appear beneficial to or neutral toward the interest of those at the bottom only when we take as given unequal structures and/or inequality-endorsing attitudes that no-one who affirms the difference principle should unprotestingly accept.[43]

A Theory of Justice is the founding text of egalitarian liberalism. It sets out principles of justice with a radically egalitarian content that it assumes can best be applied in a market economy. This is no longer largely taken for granted, as it is by Rawls, but is explicitly defended by Ronald Dworkin, who argues that 'the idea of an economic market, as a device for setting prices for a vast variety of goods and services, must be at the centre of any attractive theoretical development of equality of resources'.[44] I address the relationship between equality and the market in chapter 4. For the time being, it is important to stress that the criticisms of Rawls by Cohen and Bidet that we have just considered are friendly ones, which seek not to reject his theory, but to expose its internal inconsistencies. They suggest that Rawls's principles imply a much more radical challenge to existing social and economic institutions than their author is generally willing to acknowledge.[45]

Equality of what?

Debates about equality, Amartya Sen has suggested, raise two central questions: '(1) Why equality? (2) Equality of what?' He argues that it is the second question that is mainly at issue in contemporary controversy over equality. There are various respects in which people may be treated equally or unequally: 'Equality is judged by comparing some particular aspect of a person (such as income, or wealth, or happiness, or opportunities, or rights, or need-fulfilments) with the same aspect of another person.' The inherent diversity of human beings means that treating them equally with respect to one such 'focal variable' may lead to considerable inequalities in other dimensions. It is a rare theorist who does not favour equalizing some variable: 'Ethical plausibility is hard to achieve unless everyone is given equal consideration in *some* space that is important to the particular theory.' Nozick, for example, defends equalizing individual freedom (in effect equated with self-ownership) at the price of deep inequalities of wealth and income. Thus: 'The engaging question turns out to be "equality of what?"'[46]

It is certainly true that human diversity is sometimes bewilderingly reflected in the different focal variables that various egalitarian liberals have argued should be used in the inter-personal comparisons on which redistribution should be based. Apart from Rawls's primary social goods, the main candidates for equalization are welfare, resources, access to advantage (or opportunity for welfare) and capabilities. Considering these in turn may help to clarify not simply the nature of the redistributions proposed, but also the deep ethical reasons for seeking to achieve equality in the first place.[47]

To take *equality of welfare* first, one might consider this a modified version of utilitarianism. Both are instances of welfarism, as Sen puts it, 'the view that the goodness of a state of affairs is to be judged entirely by the goodness of the utilities in that state'.[48] Once again utility or welfare is understood here as either pleasurable mental states or the satisfaction of a person's preferences. Two objections to equality of welfare are what Cohen calls 'the *offensive tastes* and *expensive tastes* criticisms'.[49]

The first is stated by Rawls: for welfarism, 'if men take a certain pleasure in discriminating against one another, in subjecting others to a lesser liberty as a means of enhancing their self-respect, then the satisfaction of these desires must be weighed in our deliberations according to their intensity, or whatever, along with other desires'.[50] There is something profoundly wrong with a conception of justice that treats my preference for torturing you as, in principle, equally worthy of satisfaction as a homeless person's preference for shelter.

Not only do all preferences seem not to be of equal

value, but satisfying some may cost more than satisfying others. Such is the nub of the second criticism, put most systematically by Dworkin: 'Equality of welfare seems to recommend that those with champagne tastes, who need more income simply to achieve the same level of welfare as those with less expensive tastes, should have more income on that account.' In particular, what of those who deliberately cultivate expensive tastes? If it seems unreasonable to regard satisfying their desires as just as urgent as satisfying those of people who have remained content with more modest tastes, then we need to select a different focal variable to equalize.[51]

Once we start to consider the process through which individuals' preferences are formed, a third objection to equality of welfare emerges – to my mind the most important one. Preferences often adapt to circumstances. As Sen puts it, '[a] thoroughly deprived person, leading a very reduced life, might not appear too badly off in terms of the mental metric of desire and its fulfilment, if the hardship is accepted with non-grumbling resignation.'[52] This is the problem of sour grapes, or (to put it in more highfalutin terms) of adaptive preferences: one gives up wanting what one believes one cannot get. It may be particularly dangerous in situations of acute inequality and poverty to go by the preferences of the worst off, since they may have given up hope of any improvement in their condition.[53]

In place of equality of welfare, Dworkin proposes *equality of resources*. He imagines an auction in which all material productive resources are sold to individuals each with an equal amount of money with which to bid. Sub-auctions allow them also to insure themselves against being handicapped or lacking various skills. Underlying this proposal is a particular view of the rationale for equality. On this view, as Cohen puts it, 'a large part of the fundamental egalitarian aim is to extinguish the influence of brute luck on distribution'.[54] Dworkin distinguishes between two kinds of luck – 'option luck', 'which is a matter of how deliberate and calculated gambles turn out', and 'brute luck', which is 'a matter of how risks fall out that are not in that sense deliberate gambles'.[55] A victim of brute luck cannot be held responsible for the resulting disadvantage. Being born poor is one relevant example of brute luck. One of Rawls's most important contributions to egalitarian thought has been to argue that the distribution of natural talents among individuals represents, in effect, another case of brute luck, from which those advantaged are only entitled to benefit if allowing them to do so will improve the condition of the worst off.

Dworkin argues that the case for equality of resources 'produces a certain view of the distinction between a person and his circumstances, and assigns his tastes and ambitions to his person, and his physical and mental powers to his circumstances'.[56] A person can thus be held responsible for her tastes and ambitions, but not for her physical and mental powers. The latter are, like the socio-economic position into which she is born, matters of brute luck. An initial equal distribution of resources would, when undergirded by a hypothetical insurance market to compensate for inequalities in natural assets, place individuals in the same circumstances. Their responses to these circumstances would differ according to their tastes and ambitions, producing unequal outcomes. A driven and abstemious individual will end up with more resources than someone more laid-back who has expensive tastes. But *this* inequality will be a consequence of individual choices rather than the brute luck of being born with more wealth or talent than others.

Cohen comments: 'Dworkin has, in effect, performed for egalitarianism the considerable service of incorporating within it the most powerful idea in the arsenal of the anti-egalitarian right: the idea of choice and responsibility.'[57] But the relationship between choice, preferences and circumstances is complex. There is, in the first place, the problem we have already encountered of adaptive preferences. Dworkin contends that individuals are responsible for their preferences as long as they identify with them. However, John Roemer objects that it is wrong to hold people 'accountable for their choices, even if they follow from preferences which were in part or entirely formed under influences beyond their control . . . Preferences are often adjusted to what the person falsely deems to be necessity, and society does her no favour by accepting the consequences that follow from exercising them.'[58]

Secondly, individuals may, for reasons outside their control, benefit differently from the same share of resources. Sen imagines two people, A and B: 'person A as a cripple gets half the utility that the pleasure-wizard B does from a given level of income'. Neither Rawls's difference principle nor Dworkin's equality of resources takes this 'utility disadvantage', for which it would be absurd to hold A responsible, into account. Such cases illustrate the general fact that 'the conversion of goods to capabilities varies substantially from person to person and the equality of the former may still be far from the equality of the latter'.[59] These considerations also count against equality of income, advocated, for example, by Shaw, who wrote: 'The really effective incentive to work is our needs, which are equal.'[60] The case of A and B shows that our needs are *not* equal: to give A the same income as B would be to treat her unfairly.

This second objection led Cohen to propose, in answer to Sen's question, *equality of access to advantage*, where 'advantage' refers to 'a heterogeneous collection of desirable states of the person reducible neither to his resources bundle nor to his welfare level'.[61] He offers the following rationale for this proposal:

> For Dworkin it is not choice but preference which excuses what would otherwise be an unjustly unequal distribution. He proposes compensation for power deficiencies, but not for expensive tastes, whereas I believe that we should compensate for disadvantage beyond a person's control, as such, and that we should not, accordingly, draw a line between unfortunate resource endowment and unfortunate utility functions. A person with *wantonly* expensive tastes has no claim on us, but neither does a person whose powers are feeble because he has recklessly failed to develop them. There is no moral difference, from an egalitarian point of view, between a person who irresponsibly acquires (or blamelessly chooses to develop) an expensive taste and a person who irresponsibly loses (or blamelessly chooses to consume) a valuable resource. The right cut is between responsibility and bad luck, not between preferences and resources.[62]

Cohen's approach dovetails with various attempts to develop the idea of 'deep' equality of opportunity. For Roemer, for example, this idea means that 'society should do what it can to "level the playing field" among individuals who compete for positions, or, more generally, that it level the playing field among individuals during their periods of formation, so that all those with relevant potential will eventually be admissible to pools of candidates competing for positions'. The 'mounds and troughs in the playing field' correspond to 'the differential circumstances for which they [i.e. individuals] should not be held accountable and which affect their ability to achieve or have access to the kind of advantage that is being sought'.[63]

Sen, however, offers a different solution to the inadequacies of welfare and resources as focal variables: *equality of capabilities*. This idea depends on distinguishing between achievement, the means of achievement, and freedom to achieve. Welfarism concentrates on achievement – the actual satisfactions that individuals derive from various states of affairs. This is an inadequate measure of equality for the reasons we have seen above. Both Rawls's primary goods and Dworkin's resources represent a shift towards the *means* of achievement. This is a step in the right direction, but it does not go far enough. The diversity of human beings means that, as we have already seen, someone who is mentally or physically disabled or prone to some serious illness, for example, will not extract the same benefit from a given bundle of resources as someone who does not suffer from these disadvantages. The extent of their freedom to achieve, as well as their actual achievements, will therefore differ. Thus: 'Primary goods suffers from a fetishist handicap' in that it 'is concerned with good things rather than with what these good things *do* to human beings'.[64]

To remedy these defects, Sen proposes that we think of a person's well-being as depending on the quality of 'a set of interrelated "functionings", consisting of beings and doings'. These 'can vary from such elementary things as being adequately nourished, being in good health, avoiding escapable morbidity and premature mortality, etc., to more complex achievements such as being happy, having self-respect, taking part in the life of the community, and so on'. The '*capability* to function . . . represents the various combinations of functionings (beings and doings) that the person can achieve'. It thus reflects 'the person's freedom to lead one type of life rather than another'. It is equality in these capabilities that Sen proposes that we should seek to achieve: 'individual claims are not to be assessed in terms of the resources or primary goods the persons respectively hold, but by the freedoms they actually enjoy to choose the lives they have reason to value'.[65]

Most unusually for a normative political theory, Sen's capability approach has had a considerable impact on more empirical social-science literature: it has, for example, helped to inspire the efforts of the United Nations Development Programme to construct various indicators that measure development in Third World countries better than the crude indices offered by national-income statistics such as growth in gross national product.[66] From a philosophical point of view, it has the considerable interest that it seeks to relate freedom and equality. Equality of capabilities is concerned with individuals' freedom to achieve the functionings they value. 'This freedom, reflecting a person's opportunities of well-being, must be valued at least for *instrumental* reasons, e.g. in judging how good a "deal" a person has in the society. But, in addition, freedom may be seen as intrinsically important for a good social structure.' If choosing is seen as a constituent part of the good life, then 'at least some types of capabilities contribute *directly* to well-being, making one's life richer with the opportunity of reflective choice'.[67]

Sen's attempt to relate liberty and equality is important for at least two reasons. First, as we have seen, neo-liberals such as Nozick attack egalitarianism on the grounds that its achievement would drastically reduce individual freedom. But Sen argues that counterposing liberty and equality in this way 'reflects a "category mistake". They are not alternatives. Liberty is among the possible *fields of application* of equality, and equality is among the possible *patterns* of distribution of liberty.'[68] Secondly, the capability approach offers a positive rationale for equality. Rawls, Dworkin and Cohen offer effectively a negative reason for seeking to achieve equality in the preferred dimension: people should not suffer the consequences of disadvantages for which they are not responsible, whether these disadvantages derive from the distribution of productive resources or the incidence of natural talents. But one might also value equality for the more positive reason that, by equalizing individuals' freedom to achieve well-being, it contributes towards what Tawney called 'the growth towards perfection of individual human beings'.[69]

Tawney here offers a very clear statement of the ethical doctrine that Rawls calls 'perfectionism', which understands the good as the achievement of personal well-being. Rawls argues that this doctrine cannot be part of a theory of justice: the parties to the original position do not know their conception of the good, reflecting the fact that in liberal societies conceptions of the good are inherently diverse.[70] Sen approaches this subject with caution. He gives the capability approach a genealogy that includes both Aristotle, who offered a theory of the good conceived as an objectively knowable condition of well-being (*eudaimonia*), and Marx, who tacitly relied on such a theory when he argued that individuals fulfil themselves through free activity. But Sen also rejects Martha Nussbaum's proposal that he extend his own theory by 'introducing an objective normative account of human functioning', maintaining that 'quite different specific theories of value may be consistent with the capability approach'.[71]

One advantage of developing the capability approach in the direction suggested by Nussbaum is that it would offer a way of integrating two of the core values common to both traditional socialism and the Third Way, namely autonomy and equality. One might, for example, understand equality as equal access to well-being, and well-being itself as critically involving (though not reducible to) individuals' ability successfully to pursue goals that they

have chosen for themselves, but which are conceived as
having value independently of being chosen and pursued.[72] At the very least, Sen suggests that we should
value equality not so much as a passive condition, but
rather as enabling us actively to engage with the world,
and through doing so to live the kind of life we desire.

It is, however, this very running together of equality and
autonomy that gives Cohen pause. Sen is right, he argues,
to reject the welfarist idea that 'the whole relevant effect
on a person of his bundle of primary goods is on, or in
virtue of, his mental reactions to what they can do for
him'. Sen has identified what Cohen calls 'midfare', 'the
non-utility effect of goods', which consists of 'states of the
person produced by goods, states in virtue of which utility
levels take the values they do'. But midfare cannot be
reduced to the capabilities with which goods endow individuals, or the exercise of these capabilities, since 'goods
cause further desirable states directly, without any exercise
of capability on the part of their beneficiary'.[73]

It is not clear how damaging this criticism is. Sen
understands functionings to embrace both 'beings' and
'doings': that is, states as well as activities. Cohen proposes equalizing access to advantage, which, he acknowledges, 'is, like Sen's "functioning" . . ., a heterogeneous
collection of desirable states'.[74] Sen himself notes that 'if
advantage is seen specifically in terms of well-being (ignoring the agency aspect), then Cohen's "equality of access
to advantage" would be very like equality of well-being
freedom'.[75] The difference between the two perspectives
seems to lie less in what they seek to equalize than in their
underlying rationales for equality: Cohen's concern is to
eliminate the consequences of brute luck, while Sen is
drawn towards a perfectionist theory, where equalizing
capabilities enables people to realize themselves. Either
equality implies a very considerable redistribution of

wealth and income. For the purposes of my argument in the following chapter, I shall treat them as equivalent.

Writing from a position very similar to Cohen's, Richard Arneson criticizes Sen for failing to come up with an index that would allow us to rank individual capabilities. In the absence of such an index, it is very hard, given the diversity of human beings that Sen himself stresses, to compare and therefore to seek to equalize the capabilities of different persons. Arneson effectively confronts Sen with a dilemma. We can take individual preferences into account, in which case we are back to welfarism. But any objective ranking of functionings and capabilities independent of preferences presupposes 'the adequacy of an as yet unspecified perfectionist doctrine the like of which has certainly not yet been defended and is in my opinion indefensible'.[76]

Arneson's own preferred egalitarian currency, equality of opportunity for welfare, also goes beyond individuals' actual preferences. He argues that we should take 'hypothetical preferences' as 'the measure of an individual's welfare'. These are the preferences 'I would have if I were to engage in thorough going deliberation about my preferences with full pertinent information, in a calm mood, while thinking clearly and making no reasonable errors'. Idealizing preferences in this way is essential if Arneson's position is not to collapse into straight equality of welfare, with all the difficulties that this involves. But, he concedes, the effect is to require 'a normative account of preference formation that is not preference-based. A perfectionist component may thus be needed in a broadly welfarist egalitarianism.'[77] Arneson is thus caught in the same dilemma between welfarism and perfectionism with which he confronts Sen.

The difficulty that faces Arneson's critique of Sen is significant for two reasons. First, it supports Roemer's conclusion: 'Some objective measure of a person's condition should, it seems, surely count in the measure of advantage salient for distributive justice, for a subjective measure does not appear to permit a solution to the tamed housewife problem' – that is, to the adaptation of preferences to confined circumstances.[78] Despite Rawls's strenuous resistance to perfectionism, the theory of egalitarian justice is incomplete without an objective account of human well-being. Secondly, this means that egalitarian liberalism must confront the same kind of objection that is often made to Marx's critique of capitalism, namely that it counterposes people's real needs and interests to the actual preferences they have. The latter, according to the Marxist theory of ideology, tend to reflect the effect of capitalist social relations, which leads to individual desires being distorted or adjusted downwards.[79]

Egalitarian liberals may resist being drawn on to this hotly contested terrain. It is hard to see how they can avoid it, however, for their more radical redistributive proposals are likely to be met by appeals to common sense. Thus the Labour Party's Commission on Social Justice, in its extraordinarily conservative discussion of equality, invokes popular intuitions to dismiss Rawls's opposition to basing justice on the notion of desert. For example: 'Few people believe' that 'no rewards . . . are . . . a matter of desert'. Or again: 'people . . . rightly think that redistribution of income is not an aim in itself'. Insofar as the authors of these assertions are not simply dressing up their own views as what they claim 'people' think, they are making the prevailing beliefs in society the benchmark of social justice. Indeed, they declare that 'it is certain that the British public would not recognize in such a theory [i.e. Rawls's], or in any other theory with such ambitions, all its conflicting ideas and feelings about social justice'.[80]

The question of how to validate any theory of justice is undoubtedly a difficult one, but it is hard to see what the point of political philosophy is if it merely serves up the 'conflicting ideas and feelings' that happen at any given time to predominate on the subject. In particular, making these the benchmark of what we mean by social justice may give theoretical sanction to attitudes that reflect the belief of those who hold them that they cannot hope for anything better. Egalitarian liberalism cannot simply take actual preferences and the beliefs that justify them at face value. Thus, rather surprisingly, it joins hands with Marxist ideology-critique.

Injustice, exploitation and desert

That equality as a political ideal can be justified only by an objective account of well-being is also suggested by Elizabeth Anderson's detailed and skilful critique of 'luck egalitarianism', by which she means the approach favoured by Dworkin, Cohen and others that concentrates on remedying the consequences of brute luck. Luck egalitarians, Anderson contends, combine 'some of the worst aspects of capitalism and socialism': on the one hand, they adopt a harshly individualistic attitude towards the victims of bad option luck, leaving them to suffer the consequences of their own choices (by, for example, becoming disabled through their own negligence); on the other hand, they deny the victims of bad brute luck the equal respect to which they are entitled, patronizingly compensating them because of their inferiority to others. Not only does this reinstate 'the stigmatizing regime of the Poor Laws', but policing the line between 'the deserving and the undeserving disadvantaged' would require 'the state to make grossly intrusive, moralizing judgements of individual's choices'.[81]

Anderson's polemic systematically selects for the least charitable reading of luck egalitarianism. Thus she argues that it is sexist because women who are disadvantaged by caring for children would count as cases of bad option luck: 'Since women are not on average less talented than men, but choose to develop talents that command little or no market wage, it is not clear that luck egalitarians have any basis for remedying the injustices that attend their dependence on male wage-earners.' But this is a counter-example only to a version of egalitarianism such as Dworkin's that takes no account of the dependence of individuals' choices on the circumstances in which they find themselves. Given the way the highly unequal structures of our societies systematically disadvantage women, becoming an economically dependent child-carer may often be the best option available to them: Anderson effectively acknowledges the pressure of circumstances in these cases when she refers to 'entirely reasonable (and for dependent caretakers, even obligatory) choices'.[82] Equalizing access to advantage surely implies creating circumstances where women are not obliged to become economically dependent on male wage-earners.[83]

Anderson does nevertheless succeed in highlighting the vulnerability to damaging counter-example of any version of egalitarianism that is unable to appeal to some strong account of our reasons for seeking equality in the first place (she herself opts for Sen's capability approach). She does, moreover, reveal respects in which at least some kinds of luck egalitarianism concede too much to liberal individualism. One notable example is the tendency to attribute inequality chiefly to the unequal distribution of individual talents. The socialist tradition offers a different explanation when it draws attention to exploitation as a cause of unjustified inequality. As we saw in chapter 2, Marx sees capitalist exploitation as a consequence of the unequal distribution of productive resources. Workers, denied direct access to the means of production, are compelled to sell their labour-power to the capitalists, who control these means on terms that lead to the former's exploitation. This exploitation consists in the workers performing surplus-labour for the capitalists: that is, they work not simply to support themselves and their dependants, but also to provide the profits in search of which the capitalists made their investments in the first place. The surplus-labour is appropriated by capitalists who make no productive contribution themselves – or at least none commensurate with the reward they receive. This antagonistic relationship between exploiters and exploited in turn constitutes the basis of the class structure.[84]

On the face of it, the unequal distribution of alienable productive resources seems as much a case of brute luck as that of inalienable natural talents. Recent debates about equality have, however, tended to sideline the issue of exploitation. Even Roemer, who has devoted considerable effort to restating Marx's theory in a form that does not offend the intellectual sensibilities of neo-classical economists, concludes that the injustice of exploitation derives from an unjust inequality in the distribution of assets, not from the extraction of surplus-labour flowing from that distribution. He thereby shifts the focus of attention away from exploitation itself to the question of distributive justice.[85] Some egalitarian liberals adopt a considerably more negative attitude towards the idea of exploitation. Thus Thomas Nagel writes:

> an egalitarian system would have completely to forget the idea, still popular in some quarters, that the root of social

injustice is exploitation – in the sense of a failure to reward people in accordance with their productive contribution or the true value of their labour. The defence of equality requires that rewards *not* depend on productive contribution, and in particular that some people receive much more of the social product than they contribute.[86]

Part of what Nagel has in mind here (he also rejects the labour theory of value) is the fact that differences in individual talents will lead to different productive contributions; also individuals may not be able to contribute at all because they are too young, too old, too ill or unemployed. The kind of egalitarian thinking we have been considering in this chapter suggests that these differences represent disadvantages for which the individuals concerned should be compensated. An egalitarian distribution would thus not correspond to individuals' productive contributions. This line of thought is hardly new. Indeed, Marx argues in the 'Critique of the Gotha Programme' that it is its failure to take into account these differences and the consequent claims for compensation that makes the 'contribution principle', according to which individuals should be rewarded proportionally to their labour, defective, though he still thinks this principle would govern distribution in the period immediately after a socialist revolution.[87]

Do these considerations mean that egalitarians should abjure any interest in exploitation? No, because the injustice of exploitation does not depend upon the contribution principle. A person is exploited if and only if she is illegitimately compelled to work for others. One may freely choose to work for others – for example, as a gift, or where a genuinely voluntary exchange takes place. There are also cases where one may be legitimately compelled to work for others – for example, where taxes are democratically imposed to meet the legitimate aims of government (including that of achieving social justice). Slavery and serfdom are clear cases of illegitimate compulsion. What is distinctive about Marx's account of capitalist exploitation is that the *appearance* of free exchange between worker and employer is nullified by the unequal distribution of the productive forces: as a result, workers are *compelled* to sell their labour-power to the capitalists on terms that lead to their exploitation. They have, in other words, no acceptable alternative to working for capitalists on these terms. This is a violation of their liberty, even if they are not directly coerced into performing surplus-labour for the capitalist, but rather do so as a result of what Marx calls 'the silent compulsion of economic relations'.[88]

Thus exploitation is directly unjust, independently of any injustice in the initial distribution of productive assets, because workers are illegitimately compelled to work for the capitalist. Furthermore, it indirectly contributes to injustice in so far as its consequence is an unequal distribution of access to advantage. In other words, the polarization between rich and poor documented in chapter 1 may largely be a consequence of exploitation, as contemporary economic structures serve both to restrain or reduce the living standards of the majority and to increase the wealth of the privileged minority. As Erik Olin Wright puts it, exploitation is 'defined by a particular kind of mechanism through which the welfare of the exploiters is causally related to the deprivations of the exploited. In exploitation, *the material well-being of exploiters causally depends upon their ability to appropriate the fruits of the labour of the exploited.*'[89] Thus, if we are interested in the *causes* of inequality, exploitation proves to be very important indeed.

A major study attempting to give empirical content to

Marxist economic concepts estimates that the rate of surplus-value, which measures the degree to which workers are exploited, rose in the United States from 170 per cent in 1949 to 219 per cent in 1989 – an increase of 44 per cent.[90] This finding implies that there is a causal connection between the growth of inequality and poverty since the late 1970s and the appropriation of a growing amount of surplus-labour by capital. Reviewing the performance of the US economy between 1973 and 1996, Robert Brenner writes: 'the defence of profitability throughout the period, and its partial recovery in the 1990s, has been predicated upon a repression of wages without precedent throughout the last century, and perhaps since the Civil War'.[91] Wealth and poverty, and the highly unequal structures of advantage and disadvantage that they imply, are thus causally related.

It is in this light that we should consider David Goodhart's protest that 'Bill Gates has not amassed a fortune of $150 billion by exploiting the poor of Seattle' (see chapter 1). If Gates has accumulated his billions thanks to a nation- and indeed world-wide process of economic restructuring, in which the introduction of information technology has contributed to the large-scale destruction of jobs and constant pressure on wages and conditions, then he *is* implicated in a process of exploitation. The contribution principle may, by common consent, be a poor guide to remedying this state of affairs, but it does not follow that exploitation does not play a major part in producing the inequalities that require correction. Moreover, the places that exploiters and exploited have in the structure of exploitation give them interests in, respectively, maintaining or reducing inequality: to that extent, exploitation is directly relevant to the political processes through which injustice can be corrected.[92]

Exploitation also has a bearing on the question of

desert. A natural way of justifying the idea that people should be rewarded according to their productive contribution is by appealing to the idea of desert: one might say that people deserve to receive the fruits of their own efforts. Now one of the leading themes of Rawls's political philosophy is his opposition to basing the theory of justice on the notion of desert. We have already seen that he rejects the idea that people deserve their natural talents. Nor, he argues, would it be feasible to reward people according to the effort they make, since 'the effort a person is willing to make is influenced by his natural abilities and skills and the alternatives open to him . . . The idea of rewarding desert is impractical.' It is also incoherent, since it is only once we have established principles of justice that we can determine what it is that people deserve: 'the concept of moral worth is secondary to those of right and justice, and it plays no role in the substantive definition of distributive shares . . . For a society to organize itself with the aim of rewarding moral desert as a first principle would be like having the institution of property in order to punish thieves.'[93]

At its most general, the concept of desert seems simply equivalent to that of entitlement, or having a legitimate claim to x. A more specific version of the concept ties entitlement to responsibility: here a person has a legitimate claim to x because of some act or omission on her part. Arguably Rawls, when claiming that individuals don't deserve their natural talents, appeals equivocally to both these concepts, but it is desert in its second and more specific sense that seems most relevant to questions of distributive justice. Luck egalitarians like Dworkin and Cohen give desert in this sense a residual role in their theories in so far as they seek to shield individuals from the consequences of brute luck in the distribution of productive resources and natural talents, while accepting inequalities that flow from how people choose to make use of their capabilities once (as Roemer puts it) the playing field has been levelled. On this basis, I might be said to deserve whatever outcomes my actions have once access to advantage is equalized in the appropriate way.

But New Labour versions of equality seem to give desert a much more important role. As we saw earlier in this chapter, Gordon Brown attacks 'equality of outcome' for ignoring 'effort or desert'. The Commission on Social Justice even supported Nozick against Rawls on the question of desert, arguing that 'one can deserve the rewards of one's talents without deserving one's talents, and that '[s]ome inequalities are justified . . . in terms of need, merit, or reward'.[94] David Miller has offered a more systematic defence, from a socialist perspective, of the claim that 'some income inequalities are *deserved*':

> If we try to take seriously the idea that people can only deserve things when they are fully responsible for what they achieve – in the sense that the outcome was not affected by the contingencies which impinge unequally on different people – we find that the scope of desert shrinks to vanishing point. We can never say, in a real sense, that a person deserves rewards and benefits for what they have done, because it is always reasonable to assume that their performance was affected by factors for which they were not responsible.[95]

Miller's argument takes us back to the problem that we encountered above, that circumstances are likely often to shape choices: indeed, it is a more general version of Rawls's point that the effort someone puts in will be influenced by her talents. One might take this as strengthening the claim that desert is a hopeless basis for distributive justice. Miller instead argues that such a conclusion leads one to 'recommending strict equality. There will always be some external differentiating factor to account for the different efforts and choices that people make.'[96] Much depends on what is meant here by 'strict equality'. If Miller means levelling the playing field by instituting equal access to advantage or equality of capabilities or whatever, then this is, of course, precisely the state of affairs that the egalitarian philosophers we have been considering are trying to achieve. If, however, 'strict equality' means a continual process of intervention to eliminate all the differences between individuals that might derive from their circumstances, then this seems a pretty unattractive ideal, and one that corresponds to the right's caricature of what the left wants.

But it does not seem that the egalitarian hostile to basing justice on desert is driven ineluctably towards the latter sense of strict equality. There are aspects of a person's situation that are unambiguously not under her control, such as the class position and natural talents that she inherits. There are other aspects of her situation where the relative contributions of circumstance and choice are less clear-cut – for example, her own actions. The fact that we give reasons for our actions and that both actions and reasons are matters of reflection and debate is centrally involved in our being held responsible for these actions. How deep responsibility goes is a complicated matter because we are in an important sense products of both nature and society. But the case of brute luck does not seem similarly complicated: how can we be held responsible for the wealth and income of our parents and the genetic endowment we inherit from them? There are more difficult cases – for example, those discussed above of the worker and the dependent child-carer – where choices are undeniably made, but where there is a strong case for saying that the surrounding circumstances are so constraining that the individuals concerned should be compensated for the negative consequences of their choices. Perhaps we should say that these are really cases of brute luck, despite appearances to the contrary. And then there are the cases, of which everyday life is full, in which individuals are held responsible for their choices, major and minor.

The philosophical roots of the difficulty are familiar enough. We employ two apparently inconsistent languages when talking about people – one of intentional action, the other of causal explanation. One naturally lends itself to the attribution of responsibility, while the other seems to make such matters dissolve. Lurking behind these languages are some of the hardest philosophical questions, concerned with freedom and determinism. Because of their difficulty, various theoretical ploys have been devised to finesse them. But this does not alter the fact that we seem to require both these languages, and therefore also the necessity, alike in everyday life and in political and moral discourse, of drawing a dividing line between those cases where we hold individuals responsible for their actions and those where we regard the pressure of causes beyond their control as so great as to absolve them of responsibility. The egalitarian theories of justice that I have been discussing offer one way of doing so by proposing that we compensate individuals for the disadvantages that flow from the unequal distribution of productive assets and natural talents, but, having thus secured them equal access to well-being, leave it up to them what use they make of this freedom.[97]

Miller's attempt, on the contrary, to make desert one of the principal forms of distributive justice seems to reflect his particular concern to make a case for market socialism – that is, for an economy where goods and services are produced for sale on the market by competing workers' co-operatives. Thus he writes: 'If we want to show that market allocations can be substantively . . . just, the only possible way forward is to demonstrate that each participant receives what he deserves by some criterion of desert.' He goes on to contend:

> If . . . we want to keep something like our present concept of desert and the practices that go with it, there is much to be said for using overt demand as a way of measuring the value of output. Even if, from a spectator's point of view, we think that our whole social system is producing goods which have little or no real value, we should not expect an individual producing within the system to take up such a lofty attitude. From the participant's perspective, which is also the appropriate perspective for making desert judgements, it is a mistake to try to look behind consumers' demand in an effort to discover their 'real' needs (by some criterion).[98]

The circularity of this proceeding is striking: only by appealing to desert can we establish the justice of market transactions, while desert itself is reflected in the state of market demand! The contorted formulations that he uses seem to reflect a certain defensiveness on Miller's part. And well they might, for he seems to be making two pretty amazing assertions: (1) the monetary valuations that consumers put on goods and services when they purchase them accurately reflect their needs; and (2) these valuations further entitle the producers of the goods and services to the incomes they receive for participating in their production. Claim (1) does not directly concern us here, but it is worth saying that one does not require a very strong theory of real needs to know that the money income that people have to spend on goods and services may not correspond to what they perceive themselves as needing. All one has to do to establish this truth is to ask anyone in the street.[99]

As for claim (2), is it really the case that the incomes derived from market transactions reward according to desert? Let us take effort as a marker of desert. Consider workers in the computer-chip industry, which experiences very substantial fluctuations as a result of world-wide shifts in supply and demand. As a result of those fluctuations, workers putting in the same amount of effort may find that their earnings change considerably, or even that they lose their jobs because of lay-offs or plant closures. Is it really plausible to say that these changes track desert? Or again, workers with particular skills may find that their earnings increase spectacularly without any change in the effort they put in because these skills are in much demand: this has been the fortunate situation of many kinds of computer expert because of the Millennium Bug. Do these workers deserve these higher earnings, or should we just say that they have been lucky? These examples concern non-equilibrium situations, and Miller argues that 'there are good positive reasons for taking equilibrium prices as indicators of value when measuring desert'.[100] But even in the spectacularly unrealistic idealized conditions that define equilibrium in neo-classical value theory, prices reflect the relative scarcities of goods and services. In what sense can those who receive relatively high or low incomes as a result of these scarcities be said to deserve to benefit or suffer from them?[101] No wonder that Hayek carefully avoids basing his defence of market-generated inequalities on any appeal to desert, insisting that 'the value which a person's capacities or services have for us and for which he is recompensed has little relation to anything we can call moral merit or deserts'.[102]

Miller applies what seems like a hopeless general argument to the case of profits, arguing that 'genuine entrepreneurship . . . deserves reward because it creates value'.[103]

It is here that the question of exploitation is relevant. Marx's theory of capitalist exploitation does not involve an appeal to the idea of desert. He rejects the contribution principle, according to which people should be rewarded in proportion to their labour, as a case of '*bourgeois right*'; if he has a principle of justice (though he denies that he has one), it is the needs principle: 'From each according to his abilities, to each according to his needs!'[104] Furthermore, as we have seen, exploitation can be condemned as unjust simply because it violates workers' freedom, since they are illegitimately compelled to work for the capitalists. Marx's theory of exploitation is nonetheless relevant here because of the critical light it throws on various desert-based justifications of profit.

The particular justification against which Marx directs his fire appeals to the capitalist's abstention from consumption in order to fund his investments.[105] Miller relies rather on the entrepreneurial role of the capitalist in identifying some gap in the market that he can profitably fill, and successfully organizing the production and sale of whatever commodities are required to take advantage of this opportunity. Let us concede for the purposes of argument that whoever performs this role deserves some reward. The difficulty is then threefold. First, how do we calculate this reward? Consider the case of the financial speculator George Soros. Famously he made a $1 billion profit on Black Wednesday, 16 September 1992, when the pound sterling was forced out of the Exchange Rate Mechanism of the European Monetary System.[106]

Presumably this profit was partly a matter of Soros's skill and foresight in anticipating the movements of currency markets. But all of it? And if not all of it, how much? This difficulty is a case of the general one noted above. If we simply accept the market as an accurate judge of desert, then we say that people deserve to benefit from all sorts of arbitrary contingencies: for example, to what extent were Soros's profits boosted by the presumably unforeseen incompetence of the British government? But trying to separate out that portion of the profits that reflected Soros's own contribution, and that for which other factors were responsible seems like an impossible task.

Secondly, what of the cases where market rewards and contribution move in opposite directions: for example, the numerous instances where chief executives' salary and share-option packages are increased significantly, even though the performance of their companies has deteriorated over the relevant period? The justifications for such rises typically make no appeal to desert, but rather assert that competition in the international market in top executives is driving up their earnings, and therefore forcing rises on companies that wish to retain or attract the best people. The underlying rationale here is provided by the idea that, on grounds of efficiency, special incentives must be offered to talented individuals, not by any notion of desert.

Finally, what of the cases where individuals gain profits without performing any entrepreneurial function? Suppose, for example, that the decision to dump sterling in September 1992 had been made not by Soros but by a manager whom he had hired to run his hedge fund. No doubt this manager would have been generously rewarded for her services, but the lion's share of the profits would have gone to Soros and the investors in his fund. This situation is still far from uncommon. Major multinational corporations such as BMW are owned by families that play little or no role in their management. On what basis can they claim that their income from the company is a reward for entrepreneurship?

They might appeal instead to the idea that their profits

compensate them for risking their capital. I cannot discuss here the concept of risk, which has become hugely inflated in contemporary theoretical and policy debates, but it seems to me that any serious normative treatment of the subject would have to come up with a way of comparing the moral worth of, say, the risks that rich people face when they play the stock market with that of the hazards confronting workers compelled to undertake dangerous tasks in a polluted workplace because of the absence of alternative employment in their area.[107]

Miller does show some unease about the case of exploitation. He recognizes that in capitalist societies '[t]he worker's needs and the employer's command of resources together create the power relationship that culminates in exploitation.' Market socialism will, however, be different because under it 'individuals can acquire resources only through engaging in productive activity, and these resources, once acquired, cannot be converted into private capital'. Therefore: 'There is nothing incoherent in the attempt to establish an economy that is market-based but exploitation-free.'[108] But, if Miller's market socialism proved viable (a big if), this would not establish the justice of markets in general, but rather that one kind of market economy did not generate capitalist exploitation. It does not follow that market socialism would be just, since, even if access to the means of production were equalized, individuals would still receive higher incomes because of their scarce talents: that is, they would still benefit from brute luck.

To conclude: desert can at best play a residual role in any theory of distributive justice. Attempts to justify income inequalities should do so either by appealing to one of the fundamental conceptions of equality considered in the earlier sections of this chapter or by arguing that incentives are required on grounds of efficiency. All too often, invoking desert simply confuses these two distinct kinds of consideration in a way that obscures the issues at stake.

Identity and difference

There is a final theoretical difficulty with equality that has attracted much attention in recent years. This concerns the question of difference. Any conception of equality necessarily involves inter-personal comparisons with respect to one of the dimensions that we have considered above – welfare, primary goods, resources, access to advantage, or capabilities. But it is often objected that the differences among human beings are too great for such comparisons to be tenable.

Sometimes this objection takes the vulgar form of identifying radical egalitarianism with 'equality of outcome', by which is meant the demand that society should seek to place all individuals in exactly the same material situation. But *none* of the various attempts to define what Cohen calls the currency of egalitarian justice, reviewed earlier in this chapter, can be reduced to this caricature. On the contrary, the aim of equalizing those circumstances over which individuals have no control is to leave them free to pursue their goals: given that these goals differ, the outcome of individuals exercising their capabilities will also be different. Equality is not uniformity. The idea that it entails the suppression of individual difference is nonsense.

Traditionally, this objection has come from right-wing defenders of social inequality – though this has not prevented New Labour theorists like Gordon Brown and Anthony Giddens from attributing the idea of equality of outcome to their left-wing critics. But, in contemporary debates, the problem that difference poses for egalitarians has taken a more sophisticated and often a more radical form.

Two kinds of issue tend to be involved. In the first place, it is sometimes claimed that the political movements that developed in the 1960s and after have focused on a new kind of social division. These reflect non-class-based inequalities – oppression on the basis of gender, race, nationality, sexual orientation and the like. But, it is argued, remedying these inequalities does not simply involve their abolition: on the contrary, the oppressed seek to construct a collective identity that, among other things, gives a new and positive evaluation of the difference on the basis of which they suffer discrimination. On this basis, Etienne Balibar suggests that there is a limit to the dynamic of *égaliberté*: movements such as contemporary feminism represent the emergence of 'a *postmodern* epoch, in which the question is posed of transcending the abstract or generic concept of man'.[109]

Secondly, some of these movements raise the question of cultural difference. In modern liberal societies, people of diverse national origins, religious faiths and political beliefs co-exist while having very different conceptions of the good. This problem has come to preoccupy many liberal philosophers. Thus Rawls's later work, represented notably by *Political Liberalism*, has sought carefully to restate the theory of justice as fairness so that it makes no appeal to any single substantive metaphysical account of the good, but rather involves principles consistent with a number of different theories of the good. But beyond the problem of value-pluralism is that of relativism: some argue that the differences in conceptions of the good and indeed in larger systems of belief are so fundamental that no theory of justice is rationally justifiable according to some universal set of criteria. For the postmodernist philosopher Richard Rorty, for example, Rawls's left-liberal theory of justice is merely one articulation of the values that happen to prevail in American society.[110]

I wish to address the questions raised by the problem of difference at three levels. In the first place, there is the conceptual challenge that it supposedly poses to equality as an ideal. Chief among the sophisticated left-wing critics of equality is Marx, who invokes difference when criticizing the contribution principle:

> This *equal* right [to the proceeds of one's labour] is an unequal right for unequal labour. It recognizes no class distinctions, because everyone is only a worker like everyone else; but it tacitly recognizes the unequal individual endowment and thus productive capacity of workers as natural privileges. It is, *therefore, a right of inequality, in its content, like every right.* Right by its nature can exist only as the application of an equal standard; but unequal individuals (and they would not be different individuals if they were not unequal) are measurable by an equal standard only insofar as they are made subject to an equal criterion, are taken from a *certain* side only, for instance, in the present case, are regarded *only as workers* and nothing more is seen in them, everything else is ignored. Besides, one worker is married, another not; one has more children than another, etc., etc. Thus, given an equal amount of work done, and hence an equal share in the social consumption fund, one will in fact receive more than another, one will be richer than another, etc. To avoid all these defects, right will have to be unequal right rather than equal.[111]

This argument should at any rate absolve Marx of the charge of wanting to impose the same uniform condition on all human beings. His characteristically paradoxical formulation that 'equal right' is '*a right to inequality*' conceals an important tension. He establishes that the contribution principle, by ignoring differences in producers' natural talents and dependants, leads to their unequal treatment, and implies (though he cannot assert this because of his confused views on ethics) that this is unjust (why else does he refer to the contribution principle having 'defects'?). Marx further contends that any principle of equality, because it applies the same standard to diverse individuals, must treat them unequally, with, once again, the implication that this treatment is unjust.

But does this follow? Certainly, as Sen contends, the diversity of human beings means that treating them equally in respect of one variable or set of variables implies that they will be differently treated in other respects. But it does not follow that this different treatment is unjust. A person who is disabled may receive more resources than one who is not in order to secure equality of capabilities: in this case, the aim of differential allocation is to achieve equal treatment. Marx's criticism of the contribution principle is best taken not as a rejection of all principles of equality but rather as a rejection of this principle as insufficiently egalitarian, and as a call for a refined principle that takes into account all those differences for which individuals should be compensated. The needs principle might be thought of as an example of this kind of refinement. This is how Sen takes Marx's argument, which, he says, 'focused attention on the necessity to address our manifold diversities, including differences in need'.[112] We can indeed see the debate about the currency of egalitarian justice as precisely a process of refining our conceptions of equality in order to take account of all those differences that unfairly disadvantage individuals.

If this line of reasoning is correct, the mere existence of difference does not defeat equality. But what, secondly, of the argument that certain differences limit the scope of equality? Nancy Fraser has made a widely discussed proposal that we distinguish between two kinds of justice, one of which is concerned with redistribution, and the other with recognition. The first is concerned with 'socio-economic injustice, which is rooted in the political-economic structure of society' and gives rise to such phenomena as exploitation, economic marginalization and deprivation.

> The second kind of injustice is cultural or symbolic. It is rooted in patterns of representation, interpretation, and communication. Examples include cultural domination (being subjected to patterns of interpretation and communication that are associated with another culture and are alien and/or hostile to one's own); nonrecognition (being rendered invisible via the authoritative representational, communicative, and interpretive practices of one's own culture); and disrespect (being routinely maligned or disparaged in stereotypic public cultural representations and/or in everyday life interactions).[113]

Injustice of distribution has been analysed by theorists such as Marx, Rawls, Sen and Dworkin, and has been the concern of the socialist movement. Injustice of recognition has come into focus with the development of the post-1960s movements. The injuries it embraces are common to the oppression of women, blacks, lesbians and gays, and marginalized national and ethnic groups, and form the material of contemporary identity politics. Fraser stresses that 'this distinction between economic injustice and cultural injustice is analytical. In practice, the two are intertwined.' Indeed, 'far from occupying two airtight separate spheres, economic injustice and cultural injustice are usually inter-imbricated so as to reinforce one another dialectically'.[114] She nevertheless argues that it is worthwhile drawing the distinction between them in order to be able accurately to characterize the different kinds of remedy they require.

A main thrust in the considerable criticism that Fraser's proposal attracted has been to deny that economic and cultural injustice can be thus distinguished.[115] At a purely *conceptual* level, Fraser is entitled to dismiss this objection. Her distinction undoubtedly identifies two different kinds of disadvantage. But the *causal* interaction between the two goes deeper than Fraser suggests. It is not just that, typically, economic and cultural justices in some general sense mutually support one another. When we come to give an account of the disadvantages that a particular group suffers because of what one might loosely call their cultural identity – race, nationality or whatever – these disadvantages typically embrace both what one might call the injuries of misrecognition – disparagement, stereotyping and so on – and also various economic disabilities.

If we consider, for example, the plight of Kosovo Albanians under Serbian rule, their oppression involved not merely that they were denied political autonomy and the use of their language, and stigmatized as breeding too much, but also that they were excluded from jobs and university places, and that their ownership of land was reduced. Or again, the Palestinians have engaged in a long drawn-out struggle for precisely the type of recognition with which Fraser is concerned. But remedying their plight depends crucially on restoring their access to the basic productive resource – land – that they lost as a result of the establishment of the State of Israel and the 1967 war. Going in the other direction, from redistribution to recognition, we have seen that egalitarian theorists have frequently highlighted the spiritual ills associated with inequality.[116]

In the face of this kind of 'intertwining' of the economic and the cultural, one might ask: what is the point of so sharply contrasting the two kinds of injustice? Fraser's answer, as we have seen, is that it allows us to clarify the different kinds of solution to them. Now it is true that the distinction may help us to see what is wrong with certain incautious political claims – Judith Butler, for example, moves from insisting that the cultural is material to asserting that the central place of the heterosexual, monogamous family in capitalist relations of production gives the kind of cultural contestation practised by lesbian and gay activists a privileged position in any strategy for social change. Fraser's careful analysis allows her to unpick this series of conflations that so conveniently place the kind of Queer Theory practised by Butler in the front line of the anti-capitalist struggle.[117]

But Fraser's own preferred strategy of 'transformation' in the dimensions of both economic and cultural injustice envisages what she calls 'deep restructuring' in both the relations of production and 'the relations of recognition' that would be mutually supportive.[118] So, once again, the 'intertwining' of the two kinds of disadvantage seems more important than the analytical distinction between them. At the very least, this debate indicates that equality as an ideal is not irrelevant to what Fraser calls the injustice of recognition. Indeed, for the very injuries that she lists under this heading to count as wrongs, appeal must be made to some principle entitling individuals to equal recognition: it is noteworthy that among the primary goods that are to be distributed according to the two principles of justice, Rawls lists 'the social bases of self-respect'. Moreover, the causal interdependence of economic and cultural injustice implies that any serious attempt to remedy the injuries of, say, racism or the oppression of women is likely to confront all sorts of claims for the redistribution of material resources. Properly addressing these claims requires an egalitarian principle of distributive justice. In this respect also, difference does not trump equality.[119]

The third issue, of cultural relativism, raises questions of too great complexity to be properly addressed here. I simply wish to point to the existence of two kinds of egalitarian response. The first is straightforwardly philosophical. Egalitarian theorists such as Barry and Scanlon offer principled arguments that either challenge relativism outright or at least seek to restrict its scope.[120] This kind of response is, I believe, essential and entirely justified. But we can also respond to the relativists in what one might call a 'historicist' way. The era since the bourgeois revolutions of the seventeenth and eighteenth centuries has unleashed, as we saw in chapter 2, a succession of movements demanding what Balibar calls *égaliberté* – liberty and equality, understood as being capable only of joint realization.

The initial challenges to the Divine Right of Kings and more generally to authority and privilege sanctioned by tradition and prescription have unleashed a process in which different forms of inequality have been subjected to critical scrutiny and political opposition. The movements against Fraser's injustice of recognition are a continuation of this process. Inequalities between men and women, black and white, straight and gay that were held in the past to reflect biological necessity have been exposed as the contingent consequences of social relationships. These difference-based movements have widened the scope of *égaliberté*, rather than, as Balibar contends, revealed its limits.

The result is a condition in which, in the advanced capitalist societies at least, the diversity of conceptions of the good that so preoccupies liberal theorists co-exists with a generalized presumption against inequality – against the background of extensive and growing socio-economic inequalities both within these societies and on a global scale. This is a paradoxical and unstable state of affairs, but it is not one where equality can be dismissed as mere prejudice. The attempts by philosophers such as Rawls to articulate an egalitarian theory of justice must be seen in the context of societies where equality has been on the political agenda at least since the French Revolution. This historical context does not make any particular theory true, let alone guarantee the triumph of equality, but it means that egalitarian theorists are grappling with problems not of their own invention – problems that reflect something about the deep structure of modernity itself.

4

Equality and Capitalism

Equality without tears

It should be clear that the theories of egalitarian justice discussed in the previous chapter imply a considerable redistribution of society's resources. John Roemer recently estimated that to achieve 'deep' equality of opportunity with respect to education in the United States, with the objective of ensuring that children in whatever circumstances who expend the same effort will have the same adult earning capacity, would require spending $900 on every white student and $2,900 on every black student.[1]

Yet redistribution has dropped off the policy agenda, even in the case of governments ostensibly committed to equality. Some historically-minded commentators have compared the version of the Third Way practised by Tony Blair with the New Liberalism, which emerged in Britain around 1900, and which inspired the policies of the great Liberal administrations of Campbell-Bannerman and Asquith between 1905 and 1915. Thus Alan Ryan writes: 'The third way first showed up in British policies ninety-five years ago. At that point it was, and in so far as it is coherent it remains, the ideology of the New Liberalism . . . The truth is that the third way is neither New Labour, as its admirers say, nor warmed over Thatcherism, as its detractors say, but a reversion to a very old idea.'[2]

The comparison is no doubt an attractive one to Blair himself. He has frequently deplored the division in British 'progressive' forces brought about by the formation of the Labour Party and stressed the inspiration he finds in such great Liberal figures as Gladstone, Asquith and Keynes. The Labour Party, then, is led by someone who doesn't believe in its existence (perhaps not such a paradoxical situation when one considers the frequency with which religious doubts are avowed these days by members of the clergy). But Blair might find the reality of the New Liberalism a bit too radical for his liking.

The historical conjuncture in which it emerged was one where it was widely agreed in the British political elite that two challenges confronted the established order. One was the external threat presented to British industrial and naval supremacy by such rising powers as Germany and the United States; the other was the prospect of domestic social conflict raised by the emergence of an increasingly powerful and assertive labour movement. Many Liberal and Unionist politicians agreed that the situation required considerable additional government expenditure on the navy (notably the Dreadnought programme) and a programme of major social reforms to alleviate working-class discontent and improve the physical quality of a human 'stock' that the Boer War revealed to have often been greatly diminished by poverty.

They differed, however, on how to finance the expenditure. Unionists such as Joseph Chamberlain argued that protective tariffs would have the double advantage of raising the necessary moneys and protecting British industries from foreign competition. New Liberals remained committed to free trade, but were willing to depart from *laissez-faire* to the extent of supporting extensive state intervention in the economy and redistributive taxation. The latter would not only finance higher government expenditure, but also help to strengthen a broad 'progressive' coalition embracing both the Liberals and a growing but still politically subordinate labour movement. Such was the logic of Lloyd George's famous 1909 Budget, which sought to pay for the recent introduction of non-contributory old-age pensions and for the Dreadnoughts by shifting the tax burden on to the rich through higher income tax and death duties and a new duty on the value of land. The furious Unionist reaction greatly embittered party conflict, particularly after the changing parliamentary balance brought the Irish question back to the centre of politics in the years immediately before the outbreak of the First World War.[3]

The economic and social policy of the New Liberalism was thus a classic instance of what it has become habitual for New Labour dismissively to stereotype as 'tax-and-spend'. Lloyd George saw his 1909 Budget as merely the beginning of a state-directed programme of agrarian reform that was designed to break the power of the landed aristocracy and would be financed by taxing landlords' rents.[4] Blair's own attitude to redistribution is nicely captured by an anecdote from the 1997 election campaign, told by a journalist close to his court: 'Early on in the campaign, I was foolhardy enough to ask Mr Blair if there might be some small role for wealth distribution in the politics of the centre left. It would have been safer to venture he regularly beat his wife.'[5]

If Blair can claim a Liberal ancestry, it is less Gladstone in his old age, reviled by the aristocracy as a traitor to his class, or the young, Radical Lloyd George, than the more right-wing Liberal Imperialists such as Asquith and Sir Edward Grey, who supported the Boer War and took Britain into the First World War. During the 1999 Balkan War, Richard Gott denounced the belligerent stance adopted by Blair and his supporters as 'a throwback to the colonialism of the last century, when the imperial powers intervened at will in the affairs of independent states and peoples'.[6] The ambitious 'doctrine of international com-munity' unveiled by Blair at the height of the war, claim-ing the NATO powers' right to mount 'humanitarian interventions' wherever they see fit, indeed legitimizes the assertion of Western military might to maintain the exist-ing, manifestly unjust global distribution of resources.[7]

Gordon Brown, a much more traditional Labourist politician than Blair, has been more consistent in his use of egalitarian language, though the word 'redistribution' seems to have been banned in New Labour discourse. The journalist Samuel Brittan, one of the inventors of monetarism, has sympathetically described Brown's policy as Chancellor of the Exchequer as ' "redistributive market liberalism" – with only a light touch on redistribution'.[8] While Brown has pursued an orthodox neo-liberal macro-economic policy, notably by giving the Bank of England independent control over interest rates and by reducing overall public expenditure in real terms, he has simul-taneously practised what David Piachaud calls 'redistri-bution by stealth'. This has involved higher benefits and new tax credits directed at poorer households with chil-dren, financed, in the case of the withdrawal of the children's tax credit for higher-rate income tax-payers, by higher marginal tax rates for those on middle incomes.[9]

Brown's broad approach to equality is an instance of what Stuart White has named '*endowment egalitarianism*'. This involves equalizing 'the background distribution of productive endowments so that market interactions lead to a greater initial equality of income, lessening the need for subsequent redistribution'.[10] The New Labour version of this approach involves, however, equalizing access to only one productive endowment – skills – through improved education and training. Thus, while still in opposition Brown called for

> a new economic egalitarianism which starts from the recognition that it is indeed people's potential – and thus the value of their labour – that is the driving force of the modern economy, and that the modern economy succeeds or fails through enhancing the skills of everyone. Instead of labour for the benefit of the few, the challenge is to rebuild our economy to ensure labour can use capital for the benefit of all.[11]

Brown underlines that improving skills is an alternative to any more extensive redistribution of productive resources: 'where the success and failure of an economy depend on access to knowledge more than access to capital, individual liberation arises from the enhancement of the value of labour rather than the abolition of private capital'.[12] This approach corresponds broadly to Joel Rogers' and Wolfgang Streeck's argument that the left requires a post-Keynesian policy of 'effective supply', in which the state seeks to provide the collective goods – notably education and training – on which they claim competitiveness in the era of 'flexible accumulation' depends.[13]

In office Brown has pursued this 'new economic egalitarianism' under the slogan of 'Work as the Route to Opportunity'. New tax credits have been introduced to guarantee poor households with children a higher minimum income; the rates at which benefits and credits are withdrawn from those in work have been graduated to give more poor people an incentive to move into paid employment; resources are being devoted to what a Treasury paper calls '[h]elping people from Welfare to Work with the *New Deal* programme to provide new work opportunities for people who have become detached from the labour market'; and 'the Government is working to tackle inequality of opportunity at its roots' by raising education standards.[14]

While not perhaps quite meriting some of the plaudits directed at it by journalists eager to ingratiate themselves with New Labour, there is no doubt that Brown's strategy is a seriously intended and systematically conceived attempt to reduce inequality and poverty in British society. It is, however, misconceived, internally incoherent and therefore incapable of achieving its stated objectives.

The central contradiction lies in Brown's attempt to combine neo-liberalism and egalitarianism. The Treasury paper cited above stresses the importance of '[a] macro-economic framework which promotes a platform for long-term sustained growth. This will help prevent the large swings in output which destroy jobs and create pools of long-term unemployment which have a scarring effect on people's subsequent employment opportunities.'[15] As Chancellor, Brown constantly repeats the mantra that 'prudent' monetary and fiscal policies are necessary to avoid the 'boom and bust' cycle that he associates with the previous Conservative administration.

There is a superficial paradox here, namely that Brown holds the politicians of the Thatcher era responsible for economic instability while appropriating the neo-liberal orthodoxy which they were the first British government of the post-war era to seek systematically to apply. But the deeper contradiction lies in his belief (which dissolves this apparent paradox) that neo-liberal macro-economic policies, correctly applied (as, he claims, they were not by the Tories), will, in effect, abolish the business cycle and thereby contribute towards eliminating the mass unemployment that Brown correctly holds to be one of the main sources of poverty and inequality.

This belief implies the relatively crude version of neo-classical orthodoxy that holds that economic crises and mass unemployment are caused by imperfections of the market mechanism. This version is associated in particular with the doctrine of the natural rate of unemployment, demolished by Keynes in the 1930s but rehabilitated by Milton Friedman and his fellow monetarists in the 1970s. On this view, the rate of unemployment tends to a certain level reflecting factors determining the supply and demand of labour in the real economy. Any attempt by the government to push unemployment below this rate – for example, by seeking to increase effective demand – will simply increase the rate of inflation; hence the natural rate is often called the Non-Accelerating Inflation Rate of Unemployment (NAIRU). To reduce the natural rate of unemployment requires 'supply-side' measures that give employers a greater incentive to hire workers.[16]

Some indication of the kind of measures involved is provided by an unusually blunt internal Bank of England memorandum written in July 1930, as the Great Depression forced up Britain's already high levels of unemployment:

> Of the remedies proposed, the Bank prefer –
>
> (1) Reduction of real wages in the sheltered industries [i.e. those not exposed to international competition], and if this is insufficient, in the unsheltered as well.
> (2) Reduction of real social service benefits to a point where fear of unemployment is increased and the mobility of labour stimulated.
> (3) Redistribution of taxation to bear less heavily on profits and more heavily on sheltered classes of all kinds, and redistribution of social service charges so that they will not be a tax on employment.
> (4) Rationalization.
> (5) A Calvinist outlook.[17]

This generous spirit of pre-Keynesian economic liberalism still informs contemporary neo-liberalism, even if the latter's public language is usually less brutal. Bastions of *laissez-faire* such as the European Central Bank argue that the chronic mass unemployment afflicting the advanced economies is largely 'structural': that is, it is caused by supply-side defects, chief among which are over-rigid labour markets, over-mighty trade unions and over-generous welfare provision. Contemporary social-democratic leaders increasingly endorse this diagnosis. In a recent policy statement, Tony Blair and Gerhard Schröder declare: 'In much of Europe unemployment is far too high – and a large amount of it is structural.' They go on to call for 'a new supply-side agenda for the left'.[18]

Apart from lower corporate taxation, this agenda calls for 'a fruitful combination of micro-economic flexibility and macro-economic stability'. In particular, '[r]igidity and over-regulation hamper our success in the knowledge-based service economy of the future . . . We need to become more flexible, not less.' At the same time, Blair and Schröder protest: 'Modern social democrats are not laissez-faire neo-liberals. Flexible markets must be combined with a newly defined role for an active state. The top priority must be investment in human and social capital.'[19] Once again it is the enhancement of individuals' endowments of skills through education and training that is held to differentiate the Third Way from neo-liberalism.

Despite this strategy's emphasis on allowing individuals to fulfil their potential, it has a concealed authoritarian dimension. Consider the world prescribed by the neo-liberal orthodoxy outlined above. The pursuit of macro-economic stability through sound fiscal and monetary policy is expected by this orthodoxy to remove the causes of cyclical unemployment, by eliminating (or greatly alleviating) the cycle of boom and slump. Meanwhile, labour-market flexibility – largely established in the United States and Britain, both Thatcherites and supporters of the Third Way agree – will do away with structural unemployment. Finally, programmes such as Labour's New Deal will prepare the long-term unemployed for re-entry into – or first experience of – the labour market.

In such a world, anyone who is still without a job must have freely chosen this condition. The Utopia implied by neo-classical models of perfect competition will have been established: all unemployment will be voluntary. The closer we approach this happy state of affairs, the more appropriate it will presumably be to force on to the labour-market those recalcitrants who persist in remaining jobless. There is, therefore, a rather sinister ring to Blair's and Schröder's 'active supply-side labour market policy' seeking, *inter alia*, to '[i]ntroduce targeted programmes for the long-term unemployed and other disadvantaged groups to give them the opportunity to reintegrate into the labour market on the principle of rights and responsibilities going together', and 'assess all benefit recipients, including people of working age in the receipt of disability benefits, for their potential to earn, and reform state employment services to assist those capable of work to find appropriate work'.[20]

'Assisting' people into work may turn out to mean driving them there – perhaps, as has happened in the United States under the 1996 welfare 'reform' endorsed by Clinton as part of his strategy of triangulation (i.e. adopting the policy agenda of the Republican right), by withdrawing their benefits altogether. The threat is almost explicit in the Blair–Schröder document: 'New policies to offer unemployed people jobs and training are a social democratic priority – but we also expect everyone to take up the opportunity offered.'[21]

We can see the same logic at work in a recent speech of

Brown's, where he affirmed New Labour's commitment
to full employment only to reinterpret this goal as
'employment *opportunities* for all'.[22] Once again, the implication is that it is incumbent on individuals to take up
these opportunities. When Brown announced in November 1999 that the New Deal welfare-to-work programme
would be extended to unemployed people aged 25 or over
(originally it was restricted to those between 18 and 24),
the *Financial Times* commented: 'Clearly Tony Blair's
government is moving determinedly towards a system of
workfare – one that makes benefits conditional on willing-
ness to work.'[23]

Once this logic is understood, what is often thought to
be a contradiction in Third Way politics dissolves. Commentators contrast Blair's embrace of economic liberalism
with the moral authoritarianism he often displays with
respect to such issues as law and order and family values.
This combination of stances is unpalatable both for more
traditional Croslandite social democrats, who tend to
favour leaving individuals free to conduct their personal
lives within the limits set by public policy committed to
reducing inequality, and for those neo-liberals who hold
that free-market economics is part of a more general
libertarian approach to life.

But there is no contradiction in New Labour thinking
here. If orthodox macro-economic policy and flexible
markets are undergirded by policies designed to enhance
the market capacity of the disadvantaged, any remaining
unemployment must flow from the faults of the individuals concerned. Whether these faults are seen as consequences of personal moral failings or a more general
'culture of poverty' that encourages dysfunctional behaviour, it is but a short step from accepting this diagnosis to
supporting a public policy aimed at, through a mixture of
sanctions and incentives, re-educating the individuals con-

cerned and breaking down their resistance to participating in the world of work. In this sense, the accusation that Third Way policies tend to reinvent the Victorian concept of the undeserving poor is valid.

Three further features of this whole pattern of thought are worth noting. The first is the emphasis on paid employment as the road to salvation, or, as Brown would put it, 'the Route to Opportunity'. Any particular instance of disadvantage – being a lone parent, suffering from disability and so on – is to be remedied by getting the person concerned a job. This strategy can be justified by the evidence, noted in chapter 1, that poverty and inequality in societies such as Britain and the United States are closely related to unemployment and low-paid work. But it does not follow from such a causal explanation that the remedy lies in trying to shoe-horn everyone into jobs.

Most obviously, very large sections of the poor – notably many disabled people and the old – cannot realistically be expected to enter (or re-enter) the labour market. In circumstances where social policy requires that welfare recipients be assessed 'for their potential to earn', the effect may be to reduce those with no such potential to permanent second-class status. Treating work as the primary means for reducing inequality can thus operate as a mechanism of exclusion. The effects may not be merely symbolic. Piachaud notes the redistribution of state benefits in Britain under New Labour to the disadvantage of the childless unemployed:

> As for non-retired households without children, the poorest tenth of these are mostly out of employment and receive three-fifths of their income from social security benefits. Some of these may escape poverty as a result of welfare-to-work policies. For those who remain on social security, the

present policy of freezing these benefits in real terms will mean this group will fall further behind and their poverty will increase. The effect of this over five years is estimated to be an increase in poverty of 200,000 households containing over 300,000 people.[24]

Secondly, the first step on the road to salvation is education. Indeed, the Treasury paper cited above implies that the 'roots' of 'inequality of opportunity' lie in poor education. In this respect, New Labour remains at one with Old Labour. As we saw in chapter 2, both Tawney and Crosland laid particular emphasis on attacking inequalities in education. In the case of New Labour, the stress is less on inequality as such (the hostility that traditional social democrats displayed towards the public schools has entirely vanished) or even on higher spending on education, but on making better use of existing resources by bullying or bribing teachers to meet nationally enforced norms of efficiency. While this obnoxious policy is largely inherited from the Blair government's Tory predecessors, its justification has changed. The Thatcherite objectives of getting value for taxpayers' money and suppressing progressive teaching methods remain, but the overarching aim is now to provide individuals with the skills needed to participate in the labour market. In its particulars as well as its general design, the Third Way is a strange mixture of conservative measures alloyed by social-democratic aspirations.

This approach is vulnerable to the fundamental objection to all social-democratic strategies that seek to reduce inequality by widening access to education, namely that educational performance does not produce but rather reflects the broader pattern of social and economic disadvantage. According to the Blair government's own research,

- if one father's earnings are double the level of another, his son's maths test score is on average five percentile points higher than the other's and 2.7 percentile points higher up the reading test distribution.
- for a daughter the gain is five percentile points up the distribution of both maths and reading tests scores.[25]

These regularities suggest that efforts to improve the education system are likely to be ineffective unless they are linked to a transformation of the basic structures of inequality. The New Labour approach is also vulnerable because of its presumption that the surest long-term strategy for reducing unemployment and thereby increasing opportunity is to provide individuals with the appropriate education and training. As Blair and Schröder put it, 'lifetime access to education and training and lifelong utilization of their opportunities represent the most important security available in the modern world'.[26] This is what Robert Kuttner calls 'a human capital cure'.[27] It is dependent on the claim, repeatedly made by Brown, that in the information-hungry economies of contemporary advanced capitalism, competitiveness is increasingly a function of the quality of the human capital available: that is, on the knowledge and skills of the workforce.

Whatever the relationship between competitiveness and human capital, the implied claim that greater access to education will of itself reduce unemployment is not supported by the evidence. Take the case of the United States, increasing held up as a model by European advocates of the Third Way. Edward Luttwak has made, from a neo-conservative perspective, a compelling case against the claim that the decline in the workforce of such manufacturing 'Old Titans' of American capitalism as General Motors is being compensated for by the rise of the 'New Titans' of the information-technology industry. As Luttwak notes, in 1995 the New Titans of information technology employed a total of 128,420 workers, less than a fifth of General Motors' workforce of 721,000. Microsoft employed a mere 15,500:

> If the US economy consisted only of Old Titans with a very large but diminishing number of employees, and of New Titans that employ very few, unemployment would be rising to phenomenal levels. Of course, this is not so because of the vast and diverse array of services, everything from local, State and Federal government to dry-cleaners, with the huge and growing health-care industry in between. Within it, there are the retail and fast-food giants, . . . which have added greatly to the number of their employees. But there is a catch: they offer neither the superlative jobs that abound in the information technology sector, nor the plain but well-paid industrial jobs of the Old Titans. In large-scale retailing and in the fast-food chains, many employees work at the minimum wage, many others earn not much more, and only a few at the top are very well paid.[28]

This pattern reflects the fact that, as Luttwak puts it,

> [t]he New Titans can and do prosper by supplying only the world's elites and near elites – the buyers and users of computers, software and peripheral ancillaries – with very-high-margin products in relatively small volumes . . . What this means from a larger perspective is that information-technology is not a job-creator in the way electric motors (the last big leap) certainly were, displacing some manual workers along with steam engines, while giving birth to several new industries that offered much employment and still do. Instead, as chance would have it, information technology is a job 'sink' as physicists would say: it destroys clerical and, increasingly, administrative jobs by the million.[29]

If this analysis is correct, low-paid jobs are unlikely to offer many of their occupants the opportunity, thanks to education and training, to climb up the occupational ladder. Low pay will remain what the studies cited in chapter 1 suggest it is now – a blind alley from which the working poor cannot escape. The Blair–Schröder document tacitly concedes this: 'The labour market needs a low-wage sector in order to make low-skill jobs available. The tax and benefits system can replenish low incomes from employment and at the same time save on support payments for the unemployed.'[30] The income guarantees offered by Brown to families with children, by increasing the incentive to accept low-paid jobs, effectively subsidize employers offering such jobs. Whatever the benefits of paid employment, it is not clear how this policy genuinely widens opportunities.

Thirdly, the New Labour strategy presumes that it is possible to increase equality without any significant redistribution of wealth and income. Such is the implication of Blair's announcement: 'The class war is over. But the struggle for true equality has only just begun.' Behind it lies the claim I have just considered that, by enabling individuals to realize their potential through greater access to education and training, government can at the same time enhance economic competitiveness. And so, 'after a century of antagonism, economic efficiency and social justice are finally working in partnership.'[31] But even if the claims for improving human capital were true, is it really plausible that all the vast and entrenched inequalities surveyed in chapter 1 – including, let us recall, those on a global scale – could be seriously reduced without *any* noticeable redistribution? Only the naïve or the self-deceiving could believe that it is.[32]

Self-deception is indeed a noteworthy characteristic of the more committed egalitarians in New Labour's ranks.

Brown is sufficiently in touch with his Old Labour roots occasionally to denounce 'privilege and greed'. Thus not long ago, in a more than usually boastful speech, he looked forward euphorically to a second term of office: 'it will be the British people, that will be able to say, in the words of Roosevelt, in our first term, these forces of reaction and privilege met their match; in their second term they found their master'.[33]

Who does he think he's kidding? Brown is a leading member of a government that has dedicated itself to avoiding giving offence to the rich and privileged. Ministers from Blair down have sought their company, celebrated them publicly and solicited their financial contributions. Promises made in opposition to the trade unions concerning such issues as the minimum wage, union rights and working hours have been watered down in the face of big-business opposition. When the Trade and Industry Secretary, Stephen Byers, announced 'a crackdown on excessive boardroom pay', the *Financial Times* cynically commented: 'In the event, there was little behind the rhetoric, which explained the sighs of relief from the City audience.'[34] If New Labour does obtain a second term, the 'forces of reaction and privilege' will be able to rest easy in the knowledge that *they* are the masters.

These contortions reflect the fact that Blair and Brown believe that they can achieve equality without tears – without, that is, significant social conflict. But this is the merest delusion. So profound are social and economic inequalities, so unjust (in the terms discussed in the previous chapter) is the current distribution of resources, that the situation can begin to be remedied only by dramatic transfers from the rich to the poor. This may be an uncomfortable truth, and many may conclude that redistribution on this scale is politically impossible. But those who choose, for whatever reason, to settle for second or third best are not entitled to the comforting illusion that what they have opted for amounts to social justice.

On the capitalist roller-coaster

Beyond these specific difficulties, the fundamental contradiction of the Third Way, conceived as a social-democratic strategy, lies in its attempt to combine egalitarian aims with a neo-liberal economic policy. Can social inequality be significantly reduced in an economy that conforms to the Anglo-American model of deregulated, *laissez-faire* capitalism? Among the many reasons supporting the conclusion that it cannot, two in particular stand out.

First, social and economic inequalities have widened dramatically over the past two decades, at precisely the time when neo-liberal policies have become dominant in Western counsels. The fact that in the advanced countries this process has gone furthest in the two countries – the United States and Britain – where the return to *laissez-faire* has been most pronounced suggests that this is no mere coincidence. Indeed, the basic thrust of fiscal policy in the Reagan–Thatcher era – cuts in income and corporate taxation that benefit the rich and the better-off, greater reliance on regressive indirect taxes that hit the worse off relatively hard, reductions in social expenditure that hurt the poor – could have no other effect than to widen inequalities.

The New Labour government in Britain has persisted with Thatcherite fiscal policy, presiding over a fall in the share of national income taken by public expenditure to its lowest level since the 1960s, while holding out the promise of yet more tax cuts. Quite aside from the defects surveyed in the previous section, the kind of measures advocated by supporters of the Third Way to reduce the gap between rich and poor are likely to be ineffective when thrown into the balance against the consequences of this approach.

Secondly, the rational kernel in the version of equality of opportunity espoused especially by Gordon Brown is its recognition of the connections between unemployment, low pay and poverty. But the neo-liberal era has been one of slow growth in output and therefore high levels of unemployment. As Angus Maddison puts it in his study of the long-term development of modern capitalism, 'there was a golden age of greatly accelerated growth in the quarter-century from the Second World War, and a very substantial deterioration after 1973, though performance in this last phase has been better than in any earlier period since the golden age'. The annual average rate of growth of real gross domestic product (GDP) in the sixteen main market capitalist economies was 2.4 per cent in 1820–70, 2.5 per cent in 1870–1913, 2.0 per cent in 1913–50, 4.9 per cent in 1950–73 and 2.6 per cent in 1973–89.[35]

Since the period 1913–50 includes the Great Depression of the 1930s, by far the most serious economic crisis in the history of capitalism, when output fell by nearly 30 per cent in the US and Germany, what we have seen since 1973 is a fall in the average growth rate back to nineteenth-century levels. Maddison's figures only go up to 1989, but the 1990s have seen no real break in this pattern. At the end of 1996 the *Financial Times* reported OECD projections that 'annual average growth for the EU and the US for most of the 1990s will be only 1.9 per cent (compared to 1.6 per cent in Japan)'. The paper compared 'this dreary performance with average growth in the 1960s and early 1970s – an average of 4.8 per cent in Europe, 4.3 per cent in the US and 9.4 per cent in Japan'.[36] Towards the end of the decade, the American economy picked up speed, growing at an average rate of nearly 4 per cent in 1996–9, but this is unlikely to change the overall picture for the advanced countries, given that continental Europe stagnated for much of the 1990s, while Japan grappled with the worst deflationary crisis experienced by any major economy since the 1930s. In the year 2000, 35 million people are expected to be unemployed in the OECD bloc of rich countries.[37]

It is, when one thinks about it, a remarkable tribute to the role of institutional power in securing the acceptance of ideas – and to the effrontery of the free-marketeers – that neo-liberalism should have triumphed over Keynesian economics and been entrenched as economic orthodoxy during an era when the average growth rate nearly halved. But then intellectual modesty has not been one of neo-liberals' most obvious characteristics. Perhaps the most striking case is that of Russia, where the application of free-market 'shock therapy' in the 1990s led to an economic catastrophe greater than anything seen even in the Great Depression, wider socio-economic inequalities, and the wholesale transfer of the most profitable public assets to a handful of private entrepreneurs largely recruited from the old *nomenklatura*. Yet the Russian government's Western academic advisers, such as Jeffrey Sachs and Richard Layard (co-author of a book published in 1996 called *The Coming Russian Boom*), show no sign of contrition. One wonders what would be the effect if the kind of performance indicators imposed on British higher education during the Thatcher era were applied to such advice.[38]

This is not to hold neo-liberalism responsible for the economic slowdown after 1973. Its intellectual and political rehabilitation was a reaction to this slowdown and to the failure of Keynesian measures to overcome it. All the same, there is a strong case for saying that the return to *laissez-faire* has made the situation worse. Take the case of the chronically high levels of unemployment in the European Union. The orthodox line, endorsed by Blair and Schröder, that these are a consequence of labour-market rigidities produced by over-regulation and strong trade unions (on the Continent at least), has recently been challenged by an OECD study that found no strong connection between employment protection legislation and the level of unemployment.[39]

An alternative explanation of mass unemployment lies in the hard-wiring of neo-liberal policies into the EU, first by the convergence conditions for economic and monetary union laid down in the Maastricht Treaty, and then by the establishment, under the same treaty, of an independent and unelected European Central Bank with sole control of monetary policy since the euro was launched at the beginning of 1999.[40] One provocative recent study goes even further, arguing that Europe's high unemployment levels compared to the United States reflect the fact that American public policy is in some respects more egalitarian and certainly more actively committed to job creation than that of a EU now under largely social-democratic management.[41]

More fundamentally, the simple truth is that capitalism doesn't work in the way in which neo-classical orthodoxy claims that it does. It just is not the case that a market economy, if left to its own devices, will attain a full-employment equilibrium. As Hayek, the most astute modern defender of the free market, acknowledged in his theoretical writings, capitalism is an inherently unstable economic system that unavoidably moves through a cycle of boom and slump. There are many reasons why this is so: let me just mention two of the most important ones.[42]

The first we can associate with Keynes, since one of the main themes of the *General Theory* is the constitutive instability of financial markets. The same theme has been stressed by contemporary left-Keynesian writers such as Will Hutton and Larry Elliott in Britain.[43] Struggling to predict an inherently uncertain future and thereby to find the most profitable moment to buy or sell assets, investors on financial markets are liable to collective movements driven by greed and fear that can have devastating effects on the productive economy. Neo-liberal policies of deregulation – strongly promoted by successive US administrations since the 1970s – and the revolution in information technology have interacted with longer-term economic trends greatly to increase the volume and international mobility of the money capital invested on financial markets. The result has been the great surges of speculative Western investment that have first uplifted a succession of 'emerging market' economies – Mexico in the early 1990s, East Asia and Russia in the latter half of the same decade – and then, when euphoria turned suddenly to panic, dashed them down as capital fled as quickly as it had entered in the first place.[44]

The human consequences of these huge flows of money in and out of particular economies have been severe. In Indonesia, real salaries dropped by 30 per cent in 1998, and the incidence of poverty rose to between 14 and 20 per cent (compared to 11 per cent two years before). Household income in South Korea was 20 per cent lower in the third quarter of 1998 than a year previously. In the Philippines, real per capita income fell by 12 per cent in 1998.[45]

The severe financial panic that set in after the Russian crash in August 1998, and that led briefly in the early autumn to a flight for cash as confidence in the credit system vanished, strengthened a growing chorus of voices

critical of the 'Washington consensus' – the US Treasury–
International Monetary Fund axis promoting the global
adoption of neo-liberal policies in the 1980s and 1990s.
The idea of capital controls, designed to allow governments to regulate inflows and outflows of speculative
money, became fashionable, particularly after the Malay-
sian prime minister, Mahatir Mohamed, used them with
apparent success to alleviate the impact of the Asian crisis.
Even the World Bank and the IMF performed U-turns
and endorsed the use of capital controls.[46]

In practice, the limits of *laissez-faire* have been demon-
strated by the determined intervention of the governments
of the Group of Seven (G7) leading industrial countries
to end each panic. IMF rescue packages were constructed
for Mexico, South Korea, Indonesia and Brazil with the
dual aim of reassuring financial markets by lending the
affected countries the money to repay their Western cred-
itors and requiring the recipients to adopt neo-liberal
'reform' packages that would open them up to further
foreign investment. Even more spectacularly, in September 1998 the US Federal Reserve Board led fifteen major
investment banks in bailing out the hedge fund Long
Term Capital Management (LTCM), which had been
bankrupted by the shock-waves of the Russian crash.
LTCM's speculations in financial derivatives left it at the
peak with an incredible $900 billion market exposure
supported by only $4.8 billion in capital.[47] So the fund
had to be rescued, lest its collapse send already panicky
financial markets into free fall.

Such interventions by the G7 and the Fed achieved
their aim of reassuring the markets, but at the cost of
increasing 'moral hazard'. In other words, their effect is to
convince investors that they will be protected against the
negative consequences of their speculations and thus to
encourage them to take even greater risks, with yet more

damaging results, in the future. As one financial journalist put it, '[t]he extent of moral hazard is impossible to measure. But with each new financial crisis, and each bailout, whether by the International Monetary Fund, individual central banks or governments, the in-built bias towards excessive risk-taking is reinforced.'[48]

In the aftermath of the 1998 panic there was much talk of the need for reforms in the global 'financial architecture'. But one of the most intelligent and incisive commentators on the world economy, the *Financial Times* columnist Martin Wolf, suggested that the practical impact would be slight:

> The world's financial powers will neither prevent crises nor be able to cure them painlessly. They lack the interest, the will, and, given the politics, the means to do so . . . The conclusions of this painful episode are three: the new world of capital market openness is extremely vulnerable to crisis; the world can do little limit the pain of the afflicted; and it is up to emerging market economies to understand the risks they run and decide how best to deal with them. The world can do something to help reduce the chances of crises; it can help reduce the subsequent pain. But it is the people of the emerging market economies who experience the pain and their governments that bear the chief responsibility for minimizing it.[49]

These conclusions may be if anything insufficiently bleak in suggesting that the advanced economies are largely insulated from the consequences of financial crises. Arguably the most important form of moral hazard created by the Federal Reserve Board and other central banks when they rescued LTCM and cut interest rates in the autumn of 1998 was on Wall Street. The reassurance offered by this intervention encouraged share prices to rise to ever more stratospheric levels, taking them even more out of line with company earnings than they already were. While the rate of inflation was subdued, the price of financial assets soared. The resulting 'wealth effect' encouraged middle-class American households, enriched by the boom, to run down their savings even more and to lash out on consumer goods, and thereby allowed the US to act as 'consumer of last resort' for the world economy, partially compensating for the depressing impact of the Asian crisis. But, by inflating the stock-market bubble to even greater dimensions, the Fed's intervention may mean that when Wall Street finally falls, the effects on America and the world will be severe.[50]

The second reason for believing that capitalism is inherently unstable is offered by Marx. He argued that the sources of economic crises lie deeper than what he called the credit system (though he wrote in *Capital*, Volume III, a pioneering analysis of financial crises). On his account, the tendency towards boom and slump arises from capitalist relations of production themselves. Competition among rival capitals leads to investment in plant and equipment rising faster than the workforce from whose labour profits are extracted. The result is a fall in the general rate of profit unless various counteracting influences (of which the most important is economic crisis itself) push it back up. This tendency of the rate of profit to fall, Marx claimed, underlies the cyclical movement of the capitalist economy to move between boom and slump.[51]

This theory has provoked enormous controversy since it was first published just over a century ago. Nevertheless, there is considerable evidence that the period of instability and slow growth from which the global economy has suffered since the early 1970s involves a deep-seated crisis of profitability in the advanced world. Robert Brenner's major study of post-war capitalism offers a detailed demonstration of this proposition, though it posits different mechanisms as responsible for the fall in the rate of profit from those invoked by Marx:

> Between 1970 and 1990, the manufacturing rate of profit for the G-7 economies taken together was, on average, about 40 per cent lower than that between 1950 and 1970 . . . the radical decline in the profit rate has been the basic cause of the parallel, major decline in the rate of growth of investment, and with it the rate of growth of output, especially in manufacturing, over the same period. The sharp decline in the rate of growth of investment – along with that of output itself – is . . . the primary source of the decline in the growth of productivity, as well as a major determinant of the increase in unemployment. The reductions in the rate of profit and of growth of productivity are at the root of the sharp slowdown in the growth of real wages.[52]

If this diagnosis is correct, then many of the phenomena held to represent the health of capitalism over the past decade – for example, corporate downsizing, the increasing intensity of international competition, the tendency of multinational corporations to site more of their operations abroad, the febrile behaviour of the financial markets – are in fact symptoms of, and responses to, the low profitability of productive investment in the advanced economies. The pressure on living standards documented in chapter 1 – most notably the fall in real average hourly earnings of American non-supervisory workers – also becomes intelligible as part of a process of corporate restructuring designed to restore the rate of profit to its post-war peak. How far this process has gone in the US is a matter of controversy even among Marxist economists: my own opinion is that the boom that developed in the late 1990s was a relatively superficially based phenomenon rather than a sign that the long-term crisis of profitability had been overcome.[53] Whether or not this judgement is correct, historical experience suggests that any such resolution is likely to be temporary. The world in the twenty-first century will find itself on the same roller-coaster of boom and slump that it has ridden for the past 200 years.

Equality versus the market

The upshot of the preceding section is that capitalism as an economic system is chronically liable to profound and disruptive collapses in output and employment. The human consequences are severe. According to the United Nations Development Programme,

> [P]ast crises show that while economies regain output growth and macro-economic balances – inflation, exchange rates, balance of payments – fairly quickly, it takes longer for employment and wages to recover. An analysis of more than 300 economic crises in more than 80 countries since 1973 shows that output growth recovered to pre-crisis levels in one year on average. But real wage growth took about four years to recover, and employment growth five years. Income distribution worsened on average for three years, improving over pre-crisis levels by the fifth year.[54]

The last sentence quoted paints perhaps too rosy a picture, since, as the *Human Development Report* itself shows, the general trend is towards growing inequalities of wealth and income. In the light of these considerations, the idea, central to New Labour strategy, that an egalitarian social policy can somehow be pursued in the context of the kind of deregulated capitalism to be found in Britain and the US is simply Utopian. Nor is it obvious that some more humane version of capitalism can be found that will provide a more favourable environment for egalitarians.

After the collapse of the Eastern bloc discredited the idea of a socialist alternative to the existing system, the belief gained ground in social-democratic circles that world history would now take the form of a struggle between rival models of capitalism. In particular, 'Rhineland capitalism', with its generous social provision, regulated markets and institutionalized bargaining between state, capital and labour, offered a more attractive model for the centre left than Anglo-American *laissez-faire*. The idea of 'stakeholder capitalism', drawing its inspiration from Germany and Japan, was briefly floated in New Labour circles in the mid-1990s before being squashed as too radical by Blair and Brown. But the problem with this approach lies deeper than the conservatism of the Labour leadership. Actually existing stakeholder capitalism has been in serious trouble since the early 1990s. Japan's and Germany's economic performance over the past decade has been considerably worse than that of the US. In both countries, the political and business classes are deeply divided in the face of powerful pressures to restructure their economies along more Anglo-Saxon lines. It is doubtful whether 'Rhineland capitalism' any longer represents a stable and coherent alternative to neoliberalism.[55]

The difficulty of pursuing egalitarian aims in a capitalist context is, however, much more far-reaching than the question of the viability of particular economic models. Any serious attempt to achieve greater equality is likely significantly to disrupt the functioning of capitalism as an economic system. Take, for example, the quite widely canvassed proposal that, in place of existing welfare systems, every adult citizen should receive a basic income from the state. This is often seen as a way of overcoming the irrational consequences of the interactions of the tax system and means-tested benefits, which leave the poor in a poverty trap where they have little or no incentive to accept paid employment. But Brian Barry argues that the introduction of a basic income would serve wider egalitarian objectives: for example, helping to pave the way for market socialism.[56]

Philippe Van Parijs and Robert Van Der Veen go even further, arguing that 'if communism is to be approached within a capitalist context, it must be by way of raising as much as possible the guaranteed income in the form of a universal grant'.[57] They propose paying everyone a basic income of half per capita GDP, with adjustments to take account of such variables as age and degree of handicap. This 'Capitalist Road to Communism' (where the latter is understood in Marx's sense, as opposed to the caricature once known as 'existing socialism') would involve 'redistribution . . ., roughly, from those who perform paid work to those who do not' – a proposal justified by the claim that 'under advanced welfare-state capitalism, access to (paid) labour has become a privilege'.[58]

This assertion reflects the belief widespread among left-of-centre intellectuals in northern Europe that wage-labour is becoming a relatively marginal social experience. As a general proposition this is mistaken. Despite chronically high levels of unemployment in the advanced economies over the past generation, only a relatively small minority of the economically active population is jobless (Van Parijs's and Van Der Veen's claim that 'in Western Europe, the employed population contributes less than half of the total adult population' must depend for its truth on the dubious device of including old-age pensioners in the latter figure).[59]

In the United States working hours rose by nearly 4 per cent between 1980 and 1997, while elsewhere in the industrialized world working hours remained stable or declined slightly.[60] The idea that paid work is vanishing derives any plausibility it may have from the experience in northern Europe in the same period of slow growth and high unemployment, rendered tolerable by relatively generous welfare provision and a relatively large drop in working hours. This state of affairs is now coming under increased pressure as both the European Central Bank and big business demand reductions in social expenditure and labour-market deregulation.

But the real problem with the basic income proposal lies elsewhere, in the resistance it would evoke from capitalists. Van Parijs and Van Der Veen dismiss this objection: 'Given the considerable leeway provided by massive unemployment, it is hard to believe . . . that the replacement of the current social security net in advanced welfare states would dramatically damage profits (all things considered) and drive freely moving capitalists away.'[61] This is, to say the least, a remarkably naïve attitude in the light of the long experience of social-democratic governments 'blown off-course' (to use Harold Wilson's famous phrase) by the large-scale flight of capital: the most recent example is the Mitterrand administration in France, forced in 1981–3 to abandon its programme of Keynesian macro-economic policies and extensive nationalization by the collapse of the franc on the foreign exchanges.

Since then the markets have shown themselves extremely sensitive to any move by a government in a 'tax-and-spend' direction. In March 1999 Oskar Lafontaine, the first committed Keynesian to serve as the finance minister of a leading economy for many years, was driven to resign from the new Red–Green government in Germany as the result of a concerted campaign by leading industrialists. His chief crime was to propose a relatively limited shift in the tax burden from wage-earners to companies. In response, some of the largest German corporations threatened to move their operations abroad. The *Financial Times* baldly summarized the effect of this blackmail: 'Following their angry revolt over higher taxes, the leaders of German industry have claimed their scalp.'[62]

Barry envisages that the provision of a subsistence-level basic income would require 'a flat tax on all incomes of fifty per cent (which would, of course, be made higher on larger incomes)'.[63] If such a proposal were seriously canvassed by a major party with a serious prospect of holding office anywhere in the advanced world, the reaction of the privileged would be extravagantly ferocious.

It is important to understand that the burden of this criticism is not that the basic-income proposal is unrealistic. As I argue at greater length in the next section, too narrow a measure of 'feasibility' would strangle at birth the practical search for a more equal society. My claim is rather one of incompatibility: a basic income is inconsistent with a functioning capitalist economy. Part of the point of the universal grants proposed by both Barry and Van Parijs and Van Der Veen is to provide an acceptable alternative to paid employment. But this would drastically undermine the incentive to strike a labour contract on terms favourable to capital.

One of the driving forces behind neo-liberal efforts to reduce public expenditure and 'reform' the welfare state has been the belief that, as a result of the Long Boom, social-security benefits were eroding the incentive to perform wage-labour, particularly at low levels of pay. The aim has been, in the words of the pre-war Bank of England memorandum cited earlier in this chapter, to cut benefits 'to a point where fear of unemployment is increased and the mobility of labour stimulated'. A subsistence-level basic income would more than reverse the effects of these reductions. That is a good reason for supporting such a proposal, but it nevertheless conflicts with the conditions under which a viable capitalist economy could be reproduced. In that sense, the resistance that capitalists would undoubtedly mount to any serious attempt to introduce a basic income would be rationally based. The thought, in other words, is not simply that such an attempt would evoke damaging opposition from business interests, but that this opposition would reflect an accurate insight into the preconditions of profitable capitalist enterprise.

Supporters of basic income are thus left with a dilemma. Either the grant is set at so modest a level that it acts – like the minimum income guarantee introduced by Gordon Brown – as a subsidy to employers paying low wages or, if it is fixed anywhere near subsistence, it will disrupt the functioning of the capitalist economy and evoke fierce opposition from business interests that will itself have a destabilizing impact. Barry proposes introducing basic-income gradually, but – in all likelihood long before it neared subsistence level – the point would be reached where the latter alternative came into play. The correct response to this dilemma is not to reject the basic income proposal, which has undoubted attractions, but to recognize that it can succeed only as part of a wider move towards socialism in which, critically, control over productive resources is taken from the hands of the capitalists and collectively exercised by those whom Marx called the 'associated producers'.[64]

The case of basic income illustrates a more general point. Any attempt to move significantly in the direction of greater equality implies making drastic inroads in the workings of the market that would seriously interfere with the conditions of capitalist reproduction. Social-democratic attempts to rein in the operations of the market while offering scope for egalitarian policies thus suffer from difficulties of principle. Lionel Jospin, leader of the French Socialist Party, has sought to differentiate himself from the Blair–Clinton Third Way, declaring: 'I am for the market economy as opposed to the market society.'[65] Shortly after taking office as Prime Minister in June 1997, Jospin said: 'If market forces are allowed to let rip, it will spell the end of civilization in western Europe.'[66] But, how to rein in market forces without producing the kind of disruptive polarization I have discussed above? In practice, Jospin has pursued policies not that different from Blair's, privatizing on a far greater scale than his right-wing predecessors and allowing the election promise of a 35-hour week to be watered down beyond recognition, though (a shrewder politician) he has kept his supporters happy with left-wing rhetoric.[67]

In other words, social democrats continue to face the more general version of the dilemma stated above, one that has dogged them for the past century. In government, either they can avoid confrontation with capital and manage the market as best they can, in which case they must abandon their egalitarian aspirations, or, if they stick to their guns, they can succeed only if they take control of productive resources away from the minority who currently control them. The economic and political hazards of the latter course are enormous, but it is hard to see how anyone seriously interested in a significant increase in equality can deny its necessity.

I have so far justified this on instrumental grounds, but we should recall that a basic thrust of the egalitarian liberal arguments reviewed in chapter 3 was that access to, among other things, productive resources should be equalized. It is one of the great merits of Rawls and Dworkin in particular to have placed this issue, so to speak, on the philosophical agenda (though they leave open when this equality requires collective ownership of the means of production).[68] The narrow version of 'endowment egalitarianism' prevalent in New Labour circles has reduced the redistribution entailed to improving the availability and quality of education and training, but the principled argument should direct our attention to the requirement of equal access to the means of production themselves. The chief weakness of egalitarian liberalism is that it fails to recognize that achieving this equality, and indeed the other equalities canvassed by its proponents, is inconsistent with the maintenance of capitalist relations of production.

The test of reality

Any version of egalitarianism must confront the charge that its implementation either is impossible or would produce such negative consequences as to make it undesirable. One standard objection to the radical forms of egalitarian justice discussed in chapter 3 is that the redistribution they require would severely undermine economic efficiency. Deprived of the incentives provided by income inequality, economic actors would produce less, and the resulting falls in productivity and output would reduce the incomes of all, including that of the disadvantaged whom the redistribution was intended chiefly to benefit. Rawls's difference principle seeks to address this objection by authorizing inequalities that benefit the worst off.

A socialist version of egalitarianism is likely to face even stronger objections to its feasibility. The convulsions at the end of the 1980s, which destroyed what I prefer to call the Stalinist societies in eastern Europe and the Soviet Union, undermined whatever credibility the idea of socialist planning still had left. G.A. Cohen, founder of Analytical Marxism and a leading egalitarian political philosopher, writes: 'The socialist aspiration was to extend community to the whole of economic life. We now know that we do not know how to do that, and many think that we now know that it is impossible to do that.'[69] He is therefore ready to settle for market socialism, but very much as second best, since, 'while market socialism may remove the income injustice caused by the differential ownership of capital, it preserves the income injustice caused by differential endowments of personal capacity', and continues to rely on 'some mixture of greed and fear' to motivate economic actors.[70]

Even market socialism would, by taking control of productive resources away from private capital, represent a very substantial change. The critical question has always been whether the combination of genuinely collective ownership of the means of production and reliance on the market mechanism to allocate resources between sectors and enterprises constitutes a reproducible economic system over any period of time – I doubt strongly that it is. The broader issue of the economic feasibility of socialism is an enormous question that I cannot begin properly to address here. Suffice it to say that I believe that egalitarians such as Cohen are too hasty in dismissing socialist planning on the basis of the Soviet experience.

However we choose to characterize the social character of 'existing socialism' (in my view it was a version of capitalism rather any kind of post-capitalist society), the form of planning it employed required the total concentration of power at the centre. In principle at least, information flowed upwards from ministries and enterprises to the planners, and decisions in reverse order, from the top downwards. This structure made a certain crude sense as a means of securing for military-related heavy industries priority in resource allocation – the real motive for the system – but, as free-market critics from Mises and Hayek onwards argued, it produced hypertrophy and paralysis at the centre and widespread evasion and inefficiency in the enterprises. This system of 'planning' (if it deserves the word, since it was so driven by exogenous pressures from the global structure of military competition) plainly failed. It does not follow, however, that other versions of planning must do so. Yet, through some bizarre ideological mechanism, *every* conceivable alternative to the market has been discredited by the collapse of Stalinism. Plainly this has much to do with the historical context of that collapse, and most particularly what it is now convenient to call globalization – the marked trend for production, trade and finance to burst beyond national confines. This internationalization of capital goes a long way towards explaining why the Soviet Union fell apart when it did: brutally successful in mobilizing and centralizing resources on a national scale, the Stalinist system was wholly incapable of seizing the new competitive advantages offered by global economic integration.

The demise of 'existing socialism' is thus the most dramatic demonstration of the incompatibility of nationally organized capitalism with the new world economy. The further inference, made even by the more left-wing egalitarian philosophers such as Cohen, that this experience demonstrates the *necessary* superiority of the market over other forms of economic co-ordination does not seem warranted by the evidence. The choice between, on the one hand, market capitalism, particularly in its Anglo-American variant, and, on the other hand, defunct Stalinism is a hopelessly impoverished one. Yet it is the sole one offered by mainstream political discourse – if only as a way of affirming, yet again, the superiority of liberal capitalism. Now that the immediate reverberations of the upheavals of 1989 and 1991 have worked themselves out, and as the defects of capitalism once more make themselves felt, it is surely time to give serious consideration to models of democratic socialist planning. It does not seem beyond the powers of human ingenuity to devise a much more decentralized system of planning in which information and decisions flow horizontally among different groups of producers and consumers rather than vertically between centre and productive units. Pat Devine's model of 'negotiated co-ordination' illustrates how such a system might work. One of its merits is that it would require the extensive democratization of economic and social life – a development that would in any case be desirable on other grounds.[71]

There is thus no reason why socialist planning should not be consistent with an economy capable of reproduction over time. But socialism, like any radical egalitarianism, must confront the objection that, even if in principle economically feasible, it cannot be realized because of the conflict it implies with entrenched human motivations. This view is expressed, from an egalitarian liberal perspective, by Thomas Nagel. He sees this as an instance of the struggle within the individual between, on the one hand, '[t]he impersonal standpoint [that] in each of us produces . . . a powerful demand for universal impartiality and equality', and, on the other hand, 'the personal standpoint [that] gives rise to individualistic motives and requirements which present obstacles to the pursuit and realization of such ideals'.[72]

More specifically, Nagel suggests: 'My suspicion is that a politically secure combination of equality with liberty and democracy would require a far greater transformation of human nature than there is reason either to expect or to require.' Moreover: 'Economic life cannot be disentangled from private choice and personal motivations, without disastrous consequences. And the operation of such motives in the economy seems bound to frustrate the pursuit of a comprehensive egalitarian ideal however great may be the political will to achieve it. This is the familiar problem of incentives.' Consequently, we should settle for what's feasible, the establishment of a 'social minimum' financed by progressive taxation that leaves major inequalities in place.[73]

Nagel's position is, as he points out, 'the point of view behind contemporary social democracy'.[74] Perhaps the greatest merit of his argument is that it reveals this point of view's dependence on the traditional conservative view that egalitarian social change is rendered null by human nature. Indeed, it is hard not to see Nagel's counter-position of the impersonal and personal perspectives as a modern philosophical restatement of the ancient Christian–Platonic conception of the person as a complex entity composed of antagonistic higher and lower selves.[75]

Of course, to give an argument a dubious genealogy is not thereby to dispose of it. Disputes over human nature are notoriously hard to resolve, in large part because normative and factual considerations are usually hopelessly entangled. Nevertheless, it is worth reminding ourselves of the standard socialist objection to appeals to human nature in order to trump calls for egalitarian change, namely that such appeals tend to confuse the local and the contingent with the universal and the natural. Cohen in effect offers a version of this objection when he argues that incentive structures that favour the better off maximize productivity and output only given the constraints set by inegalitarian attitudes and structures.[76]

In other words, relative to the context defined by these attitudes and structures, offering incentives to the better off may indeed produce optimal results. But this says nothing about how individuals will behave in a different social context. In a suitably altered social structure, where different beliefs about individuals' relations to each other prevail, motivations other than the expectation of material reward may suffice. One example is what Cohen calls the community motivation – 'I produce because I desire to serve my fellow human beings while being served by them', where I expect my service to be at least roughly reciprocated, but do not (as in the case of market motivation) produce *because* I desire to be served in turn.[77]

One obstacle in seeing our way round the expectations produced by inegalitarian structures and attitudes is the effect of what Marx named fetishism. These historically specific structures and attitudes and the ways of behaving they produce have come to seem natural and therefore unalterable. Whatever the negative features of the Keynesian era, it did involve a considerable widening of the areas of social and economic life that were seen as being amenable to conscious control and even transformation. The neo-liberal reaction of the past generation represents a dramatic narrowing of the scope for autonomous human intervention. Once again the market mechanism has been hypostatized into a natural force unresponsive to human wishes.

Fetishism reduces the set of what is thought to be possible, and therefore makes it harder to mobilize substantial numbers of people to support greater equality. It does not follow that this obstacle cannot be overcome. The situation would indeed be difficult if egalitarians such as Nagel and even Cohen were right in believing that the majority of citizens, in the advanced economies at least, were affluent, contented and therefore indifferent to the plight of an impoverished minority. But this belief is false, as I tried to show in chapter 1. Even where real pay has not actually fallen (as it did in the United States between the early 1970s and the late 1990s), those wage-earners belonging to what in America is known by the delightfully oxymoronic expression the 'working middle class' are caught up in a structure of insecurity where – largely because of the economic tendencies discussed earlier in this chapter – their jobs, earnings, conditions and long-term future are under constant threat from waves of restructuring and downsizing afflicting public and private sectors alike.

It follows that the interests of the working majority can be mobilized in support of a strategy of social transformation. This possibility is obscured by the impact of the neo-liberal offensive of the 1980s in defeating organized labour and leaving it seriously weakened. Particularly in the US and Britain, where the New Right were most successful, the result has been a climate of political despair and social atomization: it is hardly surprising that the spurious solution of the Third Way has flourished in these circumstances.

But in continental Europe, where the workers' movement did not suffer defeats on the scale of the British miners' strike of 1984–5, the 1990s saw both an intensification of social conflict and a revival of left-wing politics. This process has gone furthest in France, where the public sector strikes of November–December 1995 represented a turning-point that pushed society significantly to the left.[78] The same pattern can be seen elsewhere in Europe, as is illustrated by the intense controversy provoked by Schröder's decision, after ousting his left-wing opponent Lafontaine, to sign up to the Third Way by issuing a joint policy document with Blair (see above) and announcing a programme of public spending cuts.

Pace the theorists of globalization, it is still possible to construct collective agents on the basis of the kind of mixture of shared interests and ideals that has historically inspired the labour movement. The great demonstration that disrupted the meeting of the World Trade Organization in Seattle on 30 November 1999 offered a glimpse of what this agent might be like, as trade unionists and non-governmental organizations concerned with the environment and Third World poverty came together to contest the neo-liberal agenda shared by the world's political and economic elites. Michael Moore vividly evoked the character of the demonstration:

> It was a massively representative body of Americans (and Canadians and Brits and French, etc.) . . . – Teamsters and turtle-lovers, grandparents and Gap clerks, the homeless and computer geeks, high school students and Alaskans, nuns and Jimmy Hoffa, Jr, airplane mechanics and caffeinated slaves from Microsoft. A few were professional protestors, but the majority looked as if it was their first exercise in a constitutionally protected redress of grievances. There were no 'leaders', no 'movement', no idea of what to do except stop the World Trade Organization from holding its secret meeting . . . Mark it down, this last great important date of the 20th century – 30 November 1999 – The Battle of Seattle, the day the people got tired of having to work for a second job while fighting off the collection agents and decided that it was time the pie was shared with the people who baked it.[79]

Despite such hopeful portents, the scale of the social transformation that is required is enormous, particularly when we take into account the structurally entrenched equalities that exist on a world scale. A book of this nature cannot offer any sort of detailed prescription. It is, however, worth stressing that the point of advocating equality along the lines canvassed in chapter 3 is not to ensure that everyone receives exactly the same amount of the currency of egalitarian justice. Shaw made the point well: 'All social reforms stop short, not at absolute logical completeness or arithmetical exactness, but at the point at which they have done their work sufficiently.'[80] What is required is a substantial move towards securing equal access to advantage. No one should be under the illusion that even steps in this direction that fell well short of fully achieving this objective would not evoke intense resistance from those who benefit from the unjust social structures that prevail today. To demand equality is to propose revolution.

The greatest obstacle to change is not, however, the revolt it would evoke from the privileged, but the belief that it is impossible. Confronted with a threatening economic environment, and with the traditional alternatives to capitalism in disarray, it is very easy for individuals to despair. It seems to me part of the duty of those seriously committed to egalitarian ideals to refuse to surrender to this mood. This does not imply embracing facile optimism that ignores the real constraints on change. But this sentiment hardly seems the main danger at present. It is far more tempting to confuse the feasible with the very limited range of options offered by existing socio-economic structures. Doing so, however, would be more than to commit an intellectual mistake. Given the scale of suffering and inequality on a world scale, it would be to acquiesce in evil.

Cohen, in the critique of left-liberal justifications of incentives that I have already cited, compares the better off who predict that they will produce less, making the poor suffer, unless they continue to be specially rewarded with a kidnapper who predicts that the child he has taken will suffer unless her parents come up with the ransom money. His point in doing so is to demonstrate the moral incoherence of such assertions when they are made by the person who has the power to make the prediction come true. They are symptomatic of the absence of what Cohen calls a 'justificatory community' between kidnapper and parents, rich and poor.[81]

But there is a larger truth in this comparison. As a matter of fact, most of us live in the shadow of the blackmail of capital. A small group of corporate rich move their money from country to country in the search of the highest return. They are able, with a large degree of success, to demand that public policy is tailored to suit their needs. Governments that threaten their interests are punished by capital flight and investment strikes. The rare offending politician is subjected to media ridicule and driven from office. But the bulk of the political elite is happy to flit like moths in the glow with which a money-worshipping culture surrounds the rich. Empty chatter about 'communitarianism' co-exists with the absence of anything resembling a genuine community.

It is time – more than time – to call the blackmailers' bluff. Their success depends on the strange climate combining complacency and pessimism, conservatism and fear that has come to pervade Western societies over the past two decades. Challenging this climate requires courage, imagination and will power inspired by the injustice that surrounds us. Beneath the surface of our supposedly contented societies, these qualities are present in abundance. Once mobilized, they can turn the world upside down.

Afterword

It may be helpful, in conclusion, to state the argument of this book in the shape of four theses:

1 Social and economic inequality is a chronic feature of the contemporary world. The available evidence suggests that, in the era of capitalist triumphalism ushered in during the 1980s by the victories of the New Right in the United States and Britain and by the collapse of the Eastern bloc, the gap between rich and poor has steadily grown, both on a world scale and within individual countries. Of course, there is nothing new about such inequalities, but they represent a standing reproach to modern liberal societies that, since the American and French Revolutions, have guaranteed their citizens equal respect. The promise of what Etienne Balibar calls *égali-berté* – of equality and liberty conceived as principles that can only be realized jointly – seems indeed to be a constitutive feature of modernity, and one that it is far from fulfilling. The pressure that this failure places on politicians – even at a time when much trouble has been taken to expunge large-scale ideological conflicts from mainstream discourse – is reflected in the considerable efforts by the New Labour government in Britain to demonstrate that it is pursuing a strategy aimed at signifi-cantly diminishing inequality. The fact that, as I have tried

to show, this strategy stands very little chance of succeeding hardly diminishes the urgency of the issue.

2 Egalitarian liberalism has, since the appearance of John Rawls's *A Theory of Justice* nearly a generation ago, greatly improved our philosophical understanding of the nature of distributive justice. The difference principle offers a criterion by which to judge whether unequal distributions are to be tolerated, namely only when they are to the advantage of the worst-off. The debate over the currency of egalitarian justice has also, despite the arcane by-roads into which it has sometimes strayed, also produced greater clarity. Both G.A. Cohen's equal access to advantage and Amartya Sen's equality of capabilities suggest that what we should be seeking to equalize is individuals' ability to engage in as wide a range as possible of activities and states (what Sen calls 'functionings') that they have reason to value. Sen's capabilities approach has the further merit of indicating that egalitarianism is driven not merely by the justified desire to eliminate the harmful consequences of brute luck, but by the objective of ensuring that all have equal access to well-being, where well-being involves the successful pursuit of goals that are both valuable and freely chosen. The fact that well-being cannot be reduced to the satisfaction of individual preference is important because it rules out the more subjectivist versions of luck egalitarianism that hold individuals responsible for the consequences of all the choices they make once access to welfare or resources has been equalized. Often circumstances so confine choices that individual preferences adapt to this constrained situation. To treat the decisions reflecting these preferences as the outcome of free choice would be to do the individuals concerned a grave injustice.

3 The greatest weakness of egalitarian liberalism is, however, its assumption that justice can be done within

the framework of a capitalist market economy. This is a premiss that it shares with the ideologists of the Third Way. It is reflected in egalitarian liberals' tendency to neglect the role of exploitation – the extraction of surplus labour from wage-labourers – in creating and sustaining the existing structures of inequality (Cohen is an exception: his concern with exploitation reflects a continuing socialist commitment). They focus on differences in natural talent as the main source of inequality – a view that completely fails to address the entrenched structures of privilege and power on a world scale. The inherent conflict between capitalism and equality is suggested by the direct connection between the various measures taken to revive profitability over the past two decades – deregulation, corporate downsizing, tax cuts for the better off, reductions in social provision – and the growing gap between rich and poor. More abstract reflection suggests that the measures that egalitarians recommend to improve the condition of the worst-off would, above all by undermining the incentive to take part in the labour-market on terms favourable to capital, severely disrupt the profitable functioning of the capitalist economy. Egalitarian justice can be achieved only *against* capitalism.

4 This conclusion, of course, poses the greatest political difficulty: since the collapse of the Soviet Union, few believe that there is a viable and attractive socio-economic alternative to capitalism. The idea of market socialism offers a half-way house, seeking to combine collective ownership of the means of production with the market's supposed superiority to other forms in the efficient allocation of resources. Even if this combination were stable (which seems doubtful), it would leave unremedied the injustices arising from differences in individual ability and need. But a non-market alternative to capitalism seems quite outside the bounds of contemporary common sense.

To change this state of affairs will require, among other things, a revival in Utopian imagination – that is, in our capacity to anticipate, at least in outline, an efficient and democratic non-market form of economic co-ordination. Our current inability to do so is a consequence both of disappointed hopes and of the imaginative dominance that a particular type of capitalism – the Anglo-American *laissez-faire* model – has acquired for various contingent reasons. What the French call *la pensée unique* – a narrow set of neo-liberal dogmas and recipes – currently exerts an almost totalitarian hold on policy debate. But this will pass. Already we can see the signs of a developing popular reaction to the effects of this consensus. From the movements that are currently emerging against neo-liberalism will develop new visions of how to run the world better. Here lies our best hope of forcing modernity finally to fulfil its promise of equality and liberty.

Notes

Chapter 1   Inequality today

1   United Nations Development Programme (hereinafter UNDP), *Human Development Report 1999* (New York, 1999), p. 3.
2   Ibid., pp. 37, 38, and *Guardian*, 12 and 14 July 1999.
3   UNDP, *Human Development Report 1999*, pp. 36, 39. The Gini coefficient is used by economists to measure the degree of inequality: the closer it is to 1.00, the higher the level of inequality; the closer it is to zero, the greater the equality.
4   *Libération*, 5 August 1999.
5   UNDP, *Human Development Report 1999*, pp. 37, 39.
6   K. Phillips, *The Politics of Rich and Poor* (New York, 1991), p. 10.
7   E. Luttwak, *Turbo-Capitalism* (London, 1999), p. 67.
8   HM Treasury, *Tackling Poverty and Extending Opportunity*, March 1999, p. 17.
9   S.P. Jenkins, 'Income Dynamics in Britain 1991–6', in *Persistent Poverty and Lifetime Inequality: The Evidence*, CASEreport 5/HM Treasury Occasional Paper No. 10, March 1999, p. 4.
10   M.B. Stewart, 'Low Pay, No Pay Dynamics', ibid., p. 76.
11   R. Dickens, 'Wage Mobility in Great Britain', ibid., p. 80.
12   *Tackling Poverty and Extending Opportunity*, p. 31.
13   T. Nagel, *Equality and Partiality* (New York, 1991), p. 90.

G.A. Cohen's arguments for the obsolescence of Marxist class theory in *Self-Ownership, Freedom, and Equality* (Cambridge, 1995), esp. Introduction and ch. 6, rely on the same assumption without explicitly defending it.

14 See also E.O. Wright, 'Inequality', in id., *Interrogating Inequality* (London, 1994).

15 G.A. Cohen, 'Back to Socialist Basics', in J. Franklin, ed., *Equality* (London, 1997), p. 41.

16 UNDP, *Human Development Report 1999*, pp. 61–6.

17 D. Piachaud, 'Wealth by Stealth', *Guardian*, 1 September 1999.

18 *Financial Times*, 5 July 1999.

19 J. Pullinger, ed., *Social Trends 28* (London, 1998), p. 100 and Figure 5.17.

20 Luttwak, *Turbo-Capitalism*, pp. 95–6.

21 R. Brenner, 'Uneven Development and the Long Downturn', *New Left Review*, 229 (1998), pp. 191–2.

22 J. Madrick, *The End of Affluence* (New York, 1997), pp. 16–17.

23 Ibid., pp. 139–42 (quotation from p. 142).

24 W. Hutton, *The State We're In* (London, 1995), pp. 109, 108.

25 P. Bourdieu, *Contre-feux* (Paris, 1998), pp. 95, 96–7, 99.

26 Nagel, *Equality and Partiality*, p. 5.

27 D. Goodhart, 'Don't Mind the Gap', *Prospect*, August/ September 1999, p. 12. But compare Michael Prowse's much more thoughtful piece, 'Mind the Gap', *Prospect*, January 2000.

28 Quoted, D. Healey, *The Time of My Life* (London, 1990), p. 369. Healey denies, however, that he said he planned to 'squeeze the rich till the pips squeak'.

29 'Europe: The Third Way/*Die Neue Mitte* – Tony Blair and Gerhard Schröder', 8 June 1999, www.labour.org.uk, p. 5.

30 N. Bobbio, *Left and Right* (Cambridge, 1996), pp. 60, 82.

31 Though I do not accept his argument in its totality. Thus Bobbio claims that cutting across the distinction between left and right is one that unites extreme left and right

against moderate left and right in, respectively, opposition to and support for democracy and freedom: see ibid., pp. 20ff. This begs important questions raised by Bobbio's earlier writings on socialism: for a contrasting view of the relationship between socialism and different forms of democracy, see A. Callinicos, *The Revenge of History* (Cambridge, 1991), ch. 4.

32 T. Blair, Speech to the Labour Party Conference, 28 September 1999, www.lab.org.uk, p. 4.

33 Rawls himself says his 'two principles [of justice] express an egalitarian form of liberalism', *Political Liberalism* (expanded edn, New York, 1996), p. 6. See also R. Dworkin (1978) 'Liberalism', reprinted in M. Sandel, ed., *Liberalism and its Critics* (Oxford, 1984).

34 For a discussion and proposed explanation of this contrast, see S. Scheffler, 'Responsibility, Reactive Attitudes, and Liberalism in Philosophy and Politics', *Philosophy & Public Affairs*, 21 (1992).

35 J. Bidet, *Théorie générale* (Paris, 1999), p. 9.

36 B. Barry, *Justice as Impartiality* (Oxford, 1995), p. 214.

37 J. Lloyd, 'Prepare Ye the Way of Blair', *New Statesman*, 10 May 1999, p. 25.

38 K. Marx, *Capital*, I (Harmondsworth, 1976), p. 90.

39 Indeed, two of the theorists listed above as egalitarian liberals – Cohen and Roemer – have a Marxist background. They are leading representatives of the current known as Analytical Marxism. I am fairly sceptical about this group's claim to be renewing the Marxist tradition, but this does not diminish the interest of Cohen's and Roemer's contributions as normative political philosophers.

40 To this extent Andrew Gamble is right to say that 'Marxism does not represent the negation of liberalism so much as the attempt to fulfil it': 'Why Bother with Marxism?', in A. Gamble et al., eds, *Marxism and Social Science* (Houndmills, 1999), p. 4.

Chapter 2   Equality and the revolution

1   Quoted, C. Hill, *The Century of Revolution, 1603–1714* (London, 1969), p. 119.
2   T. Jefferson, *Writings* (New York, 1984), pp. 19, 1517 (letter to Weightman, 24 June 1826).
3   For more on Tocqueville's analysis of modernity, see A. Callinicos, *Social Theory* (Cambridge, 1999), pp. 67–72.
4   Boswell, *Life of Johnson* (Oxford, 1980), p. 876.
5   E. Balibar, ' "Droits de l'homme" et "droits du citoyen": La Dialectique moderne de l'égalité et de la liberté', *Actuel Marx*, 8 (1990), pp. 20, 21, 22.
6   Ibid., p. 23. Balibar here cites Marx's affirmation: 'The emancipation of the working class is conquered by the working classes themselves': Marx and Engels, *Selected Correspondence* (Moscow, 1965), p. 327.
7   Balibar, ' "Droits de l'homme" et "droits de citoyen" ', p. 23.
8   J. Bidet, *Théorie générale* (Paris, 1999), pp. 34, 35.
9   Ibid., p. 38.
10 K. Marx, *Capital* (3 vols, Harmondsworth, 1976–81), I, p. 152.
11 Bidet argues that to start with social structures rather than the metastructure is to reduce contractuality to 'an "ideological superstructure", . . . a simple surface form concealing the real relations (of force)': *Théorie générale*, p. 34 n. 11 (see also ibid., pp. 146–7). But there is no contradiction between insisting that modern societies must be analysed primarily in terms of their inegalitarian structures and accepting 'the proposition of *égaliberté*' – and more generally some version of egalitarian normative theory – as having whatever truth ethical sentences generally possess. Such, indeed, is the position I take in this book.
12 T. Zeldin, *France 1848–1945: Ambition and Love* (Oxford, 1979), pp. 199–200.
13 K. Marx, *Capital*, I, p. 280.
14 Ibid., pp. 279, 272–3, 382.

15 K. Marx, 'Critique of the Gotha Programme', in Marx and Engels, *Collected Works*, XXIV (London, 1989), p. 87.

16 Marx, *Grundrisse* (Harmondsworth, 1973), p. 705. See G.A. Cohen, Review of A. Wood, *Karl Marx*, *Mind*, 92 (1983).

17 N. Geras, 'The Controversy about Marx and Justice', in A. Callinicos, ed., *Marxist Theory* (Oxford, 1989), p. 245. See also the useful discussion in J. Elster, *Making Sense of Marx* (Cambridge, 1985), ch. 4.

18 Marx, 'Critique of the Gotha Programme', p. 87.

19 Marx, *Capital*, III, p. 911. See Geras, 'The Controversy about Marx and Justice', pp. 255–6.

20 G.B. Shaw, *The Intelligent Woman's Guide to Socialism and Capitalism* (London, 1928), p. 19.

21 R.H. Tawney, *Equality* (4th edn, London, 1952), p. 36. See, on Burt, S.J. Gould, *The Mismeasure of Man* (Harmondsworth, 1984).

22 Tawney, *Equality*, pp. 84, 111, 117.

23 Ibid., pp. 118, 126–7. See also pp. 208–9 for Tawney's more detailed criteria for taking industries into public ownership.

24 C.A.R. Crosland, *The Future of Socialism* (London, 1956), p. 113.

25 Ibid., pp. 205, 214, 208, 209, 210–11. See also ibid., pp. 296ff. I have rearranged the order of Crosland's arguments.

26 Ibid., pp. 520–4 (quotation from p. 524).

27 Tawney, *Equality*, p. 157.

28 See, for example, C. Price, 'Education Secretary', in D. Leonard, ed., *Crosland and New Labour* (Houndmills, 1999).

Chapter 3   Equality and the philosophers

1 G. Brown, 'Equality – Then and Now', in D. Leonard, ed., *Crosland and New Labour* (Houndmills, 1999), p. 37.

Considerable efforts are indeed made by Brown and other contributors to this collection to claim Crosland for New Labour. Raymond Plant's judicious essay – 'Crosland, Equality and New Labour' – rather stresses the differences.

2 C.A.R. Crosland, *The Future of Socialism* (London, 1956), pp. 101–3 (quotation from p. 101).

3 'Europe: The Third Way/*Die Neue Mitte* – Tony Blair and Gerhard Schröder', 8 June 1999, www.labour.org.uk, p. 1.

4 A. Carling, 'New Labour's Polity', *Imprints*, 3 (1999), p. 217. See also G.A. Cohen, *Self-Ownership, Freedom, and Equality* (Cambridge, 1995), pp. 260–2, and A. Carling, 'What Do Socialists Want?', in M. Cowling, ed., *Marxism, the Millennium and Beyond* (Houndmills, forthcoming). I am grateful to the author for supplying me the latter paper prior to publication.

5 It is perhaps worth making clear that I do not believe socialism can be *reduced* to a set of values. In the Marxist tradition it is conceived as a social system – or, more precisely – as the transitional formation connecting two modes of production, capitalism and communism. But this formation can also be seen as realizing the values listed above.

6 Brian Barry argues against identifying socialism with equality: 'If taken as fundamental equality – the equal claim to consideration of all human beings – it does not distinguish socialism from liberalism or indeed from most (non-racist) forms of modern conservatism. If taken as material equality, it is also inaccurate since very few socialists have ever been or are now in favour of complete material equality': *Does Society Exist?* (London, 1989), p. 17. But since Barry goes on to suggest that 'relative equality' is 'a theorem derivable from an adequate account of social justice', his definition of socialism as 'social justice plus collectivism' doesn't seem to differ significantly from two of the values listed by Carling – equality and community.

7 G. Brown, 'In the Real World', *Guardian*, 2 August 1996.

8 J. Lloyd, 'Iron Will, Steely Intellect', *New Statesman & Society*, 24 May 1996, p. 8.

9 See, for example, Andrew Hacker's systematic survey of black disadvantage in *Two Nations* (New York, 1993).

10 Carling, 'New Labour's Polity', p. 233. See also J. Roemer, *Equality of Opportunity* (Cambridge, MA, 1998), p. 1.

11 Brown, 'Equality', pp. 43, 44.

12 A. Giddens, *The Third Way* (Cambridge, 1998), p. 103.

13 Carling, 'New Labour's Polity', p. 234 n. 40.

14 Ibid., pp. 233, 234. Aside from Carling's excellent critique, further discussion of Giddens's *The Third Way* will be found in A. Callinicos, 'Social Theory Put to the Test of Politics: Pierre Bourdieu and Anthony Giddens', *New Left Review*, 236 (1999), pp. 79–85.

15 A. Giddens, 'Why the Old Left is Wrong on Equality', *New Statesman*, 25 October 1999, p. 25.

16 G.A. Cohen, 'Back to Socialist Basics', originally published in *New Left Review*, 207 (1994), but cited here according to the reprint in J. Franklin, ed., *Equality* (London, 1997), p. 34. See also later in this chapter.

17 Lloyd, 'Iron Will, Steely Intellect', p. 9.

18 J. Bentham, *An Introduction to the Principles of Morals and Legislation* (London, 1982), pp. 12–13.

19 J.S. Mill and J. Bentham, *Utilitarianism and Other Essays* (A. Ryan, ed., Harmondsworth, 1987), p. 336.

20 J. Rawls, *A Theory of Justice* (Oxford, 1972), p. 26.

21 Ibid., pp. 26–7.

22 H.J. Paton, *The Moral Law: Kant's Groundwork of the Metaphysics of Morals* (London, 1972), p. 71. See also Rawls, *Theory of Justice*, pp. 179–83.

23 R. Nozick, *Anarchy, State, and Utopia* (Oxford, 1974), pp. 31, 32.

24 B. Barry, *Justice as Impartiality* (Oxford, 1995), p. 201. It is therefore misleading to describe Rawls, as Michael Sandel does, as the exponent of a 'rights-based ethic': see Introduction to M. Sandel, ed., *Liberalism and Its Critics* (Oxford, 1984), pp. 3ff.

25 Rawls, *Theory of Justice*, p. 137.

26   Ibid., p. 128.

27   J. Rawls, *Political Liberalism* (expanded edn; New York, 1996), p. 258.

28   Ibid., p. 181.

29   Rawls, *Theory of Justice*, p. 302.

30   See, in addition to Barry, *Justice as Impartiality*, T. Nagel, *Equality and Partiality* (New York, 1991), and now T.M. Scanlon, *What We Owe to Each Other* (Cambridge, MA, 1998).

31   Rawls, *Theory of Justice*, pp. 62, 303.

32   Ibid., pp. 311–12, 101–2. The normative question of whether individuals are entitled to their natural talents is, as far as I can see, independent of the causal problem of the relative importance of genetic endowment and social environment in producing these talents in the first place.

33   Nozick, *Anarchy, State, and Utopia*, pp. 183–230. Nozick's critique of Rawls in fact depends on what Cohen calls 'the thesis of self-ownership, which says that each person is the morally rightful owner of his own person and powers, and, *consequently*, that each is free (morally speaking) to use those powers as he wishes, so long as he does not deploy them aggressively against others.' See, for extensive critical discussion of this thesis, Cohen, *Self-Ownership, Freedom, and Equality* (quotation from p. 67).

34   Rawls, *Theory of Justice*, p. 244. See also ibid., pp. 541–8.

35   Ibid., pp. 225, 226.

36   M.-A. Waters, ed., *Rosa Luxemburg Speaks* (New York, 1970), p. 393.

37   Rawls, *Political Liberalism*, pp. lviii n. 34, lviii–lxix. The first two conditions of liberal conceptions of justice are the liberties themselves and the 'special priority' given them: ibid., p. xlviii. All these passages come from the 1995 Introduction to the paperback edition. Rawls includes the same list of conditions (a)–(e) in his recent *The Law of Peoples* (Cambridge, MA, 1999), p. 50, a text that otherwise does seem to represent a retreat from his earlier, more universalist claims.

38   J. Bidet, *John Rawls et la théorie de la justice* (Paris, 1995),
     p. 26.
39   Rawls, *Theory of Justice*, p. 66.
40   Bidet, *John Rawls*, pp. 26, 27.
41   Rawls, *Theory of Justice*, p. 78.
42   G.A. Cohen, 'Incentives, Inequality, and Community', in
     G.B. Peterson, ed., *The Tanner Lectures on Human Values*,
     XIII (Salt Lake City, 1992). Rawls himself sees an import-
     ant connection between the difference principle and the
     idea of fraternity: *Theory of Justice*, pp. 105–6.
43   Cohen, 'Incentives, Inequality, and Community',
     pp. 269–70.
44   R. Dworkin, 'What is Equality? Part 2: Equality of
     Resources', *Philosophy and Public Affairs*, 10 (1981),
     p. 284.
45   Though the defiant tone of Rawls's response to criticisms
     of his theory for being 'abstract and unwordly' indicates
     some awareness of this challenge: see, for example, *Politi-
     cal Liberalism*, pp. lx–lxii.
46   A. Sen, *Inequality Reexamined* (Oxford, 1992), pp. 12, 1,
     3, 4. Sen first presented the issue in these terms in a
     celebrated 1980 lecture, 'Equality of What?', reprinted in
     id., *Choice, Welfare and Measurement* (Oxford, 1982). As
     so often, Aristotle made the point first: 'Justice is held by
     all to be a certain equality . . . But equality in what sort of
     things and inequality in what sort of things – that should
     not be overlooked': *The Politics* (Chicago 1985), 3.12,
     p. 103. I am grateful to Gordon Finlayson for this refer-
     ence. It is, incidentally, a striking indication of the gap
     that continues to separate Anglophone from Continental
     intellectual culture, that Bobbio (and his translator)
     should apparently believe Sen to be a woman: see *Left and
     Right* (Cambridge, 1996), p. 112 n. 3.
47   J. Roemer, *Theories of Distributive Justice* (Cambridge MA,
     1996), chs 5–8, offers a lucid introduction to recent
     debates, albeit one accompanied by much axiomatic econ-
     omic theorizing. I have also benefited from reading a
     helpful survey, M. Clayton and A. Williams, 'Egalitarian

Justice and Interpersonal Comparison', *Morell Studies in Toleration*, Discussion Paper Series No. 146, University of York, April 1999.

48 Sen, 'Equality of What?', p. 359.

49 G.A. Cohen, 'The Currency of Egalitarian Justice', *Ethics*, 99 (1989), p. 912.

50 Rawls, *Theory*, pp. 30–1.

51 R. Dworkin, 'What is Equality? Part 1: Equality of Welfare', *Philosophy and Public Affairs*, 10 (1981), pp. 228–40 (quotation from p. 228).

52 Sen, *Inequality Reexamined*, p. 55.

53 See J. Elster, *Sour Grapes* (Cambridge, 1983). Roemer is the egalitarian theorist who has had the merit of most strongly stressing this problem, though he tends towards an excessively determinist view of the relationship between circumstances and preferences, arguing that 'every individual in society can be represented as a vector of circumstances': *Theories of Distributive Justice*, p. 242.

54 Cohen, 'Currency of Egalitarian Justice', p. 931.

55 Dworkin, 'Equality of Resources', p. 292.

56 Ibid., p. 302.

57 Cohen, 'Currency of Egalitarian Justice', p. 933.

58 Roemer, *Equality of Opportunity*, pp. 19, 20. See also *Theories of Distributive Justice*, ch. 7.

59 Sen, 'Equality of What?', pp. 357, 365, 368.

60 G.B. Shaw, *The Intelligent Woman's Guide to Socialism and Capitalism* (London, 1928), p. xiv. In fact, Shaw acknowledges individual differences to the extent of proposing that those doing less attractive work should be compensated with more leisure: ibid., pp. 77–9.

61 G.A. Cohen, 'Equality of What? On Welfare, Goods, and Capabilities', in M. Nussbaum and A. Sen, eds, *The Quality of Life* (Oxford, 1993), p. 28.

62 Id., 'Currency of Egalitarian Justice', p. 922.

63 Roemer, *Equality of Opportunity*, pp. 1, 5.

64 Sen, 'Equality of What?', p. 368. See also, for example, id., *Inequality Reexamined*, pp. 27ff and 73–87.

65 Id., *Inequality Reexamined*, pp. 39–40, 81.

66 See, for example, United Nations Development Programme, *Human Development Report 1999* (New York, 1999), pp. 127–246.

67 Sen, *Inequality Reexamined*, p. 41.

68 Ibid., pp. 22–3.

69 R.H. Tawney, *Equality* (4th edn; London, 1952), p. 84.

70 Rawls, *Theory of Justice*, pp. 325–32.

71 A. Sen, 'Capability and Well-Being', in Sen and Nussbaum, eds, *The Quality of Life*, pp. 47–8. See also M. Nussbaum, 'Non-Relative Virtues: An Aristotelian Approach', in the same volume, and R.W. Miller, 'Marx and Aristotle: A Kind of Consequentialism', in A. Callinicos, ed., *Marxist Theory* (Oxford, 1989).

72 For an account of well-being in these terms, albeit one critical of egalitarianism, see J. Raz, *The Morality of Freedom* (Oxford, 1986).

73 Cohen, 'Equality of What?', p. 18. See also id., 'Amartya Sen's Unequal World', *New Left Review*, 203 (1994).

74 Cohen, 'Equality of What?', p. 28. See also id., 'Currency of Egalitarian Justice', pp. 920–1.

75 Sen, 'Capability and Well-Being', p. 46.

76 R. Arneson, 'Equality and Equal Opportunity for Welfare', *Philosophical Studies*, 56 (1989), pp. 90–2 (quotation from p. 92).

77 Ibid., pp. 82, 83, 93 n. 19. See Roemer, *Theories of Distributive Justice*, p. 268. In a more recent comment on Elizabeth Anderson's attack on 'luck egalitarianism' (see the next section), Arneson goes so far as to make the fundamental yardstick of distributive justice well-being, understood as 'achievement of what is objectively worthwhile or choiceworthy in human life' (p. 2): http://www.brown.edu/Departments/Philosophy/bears/9904arne.html. See also R. Arneson, 'Equality of Opportnity For Welfare Defended and Recanted', *Journal of Political Philosophy*, 7 (1999).

78 Roemer, *Theories of Distributive Justice*, p. 309.

79 For further discussion of these issues, see A. Callinicos, *Making History* (Cambridge, 1987), ch. 3.

80 Commission on Social Justice, *The Justice Gap* (London, 1993), pp. 13, 6. David Miller has recently sought to offer a more careful defence of such a conception of political philosophy, arguing that 'a normative theory of justice . . . is to be tested, in part, by its correspondence with our evidence concerning everyday beliefs about justice. Seen in this way, a theory of justice brings out the deep structure of a set of everyday beliefs that, on the surface, are to some degree ambiguous, confused, and contradictory': *Principles of Social Justice* (Cambridge, MA, 1999), p. 51. But, as he himself notes, his approach is vulnerable to the objection that 'to see justice in this way is to abandon its most basic critical function; our theory cannot judge an entire society, *including its beliefs*, to be radically unjust' (p. 279 n. 16). Exactly. In fact the theory of justice Miller outlines in this book goes a long way beyond the common-sense beliefs it supposedly articulates. To that extent, he cannot simply appeal to these beliefs to corroborate his theory. Miller, in other words, is in the same boat as Rawls and other egalitarian liberals whom he criticizes for seeking to revise our intuitions about justice.

81 E.S. Anderson, 'What is the Point of Equality?', *Ethics*, 109 (1999), pp. 308, 311, 310.

82 Ibid., pp. 297–8, 301.

83 Anderson's critique also suffers from apparent inconsistencies. She is rightly critical of both resource and welfare egalitarians for giving 'subjective preferences a central role in the measurement of equality' (ibid., p. 294), but taxes them with paternalism when they seek to protect individuals from some of the harmful consequences of their choices (pp. 300–1). Yet, as we have seen in the previous section, any critical political theory must acknowledge that individuals' actual preferences are not always an accurate guide to their interests. Anderson herself makes the same point: 'If individuals find happiness in their lives despite being oppressed by others, this hardly justifies continuing the oppression,' ibid, p. 304.

84 Marx argues that capitalists may make a productive con-

tribution in so far as they perform the function of superintendence and management required by any productive process, but this function is not inherent in the nature of capital, and the revenue the latter receives is not a reward for performing this function: see *Capital*, I. (Harmondsworth, 1976), pp. 448–51.

85 J. Roemer, 'Should Marxists be Interested in Exploitation?', in id., ed., *Analytical Marxism* (Cambridge, 1986). See also J. Roemer, *A General Theory of Exploitation and Class* (Cambridge, MA, 1982) and *Free to Lose* (London, 1989).

86 Nagel, *Equality and Partiality*, pp. 98–9.

87 Marx, 'Critique of the Gotha Programme', in Marx and Engels, *Collected Works*, XXIV (London, 1989), p. 86. See also the next section.

88 Marx, *Capital*, I, p. 898. See also G.A. Cohen, 'The Structure of Proletarian Unfreedom', in Roemer, ed., *Analytical Marxism*, and *Self-Ownership, Freedom, and Equality*, ch. 8, and J. Elster, *Making Sense of Marx* (Cambridge, 1985), ch. 4. I must confess my bafflement that, despite the great lucidity displayed in the two essays cited, Cohen should, for much of the book of which the second essay is part, entangle himself in tortuous arguments intended to deal with the bizarre connection he sees between Marx's theory of exploitation and the libertarian idea, shared by Nozick and Locke, that individuals own themselves. For a splendidly sensible deflation of these arguments, see B. Barry, 'You Have to be Crazy to Believe It', *Times Literary Supplement*, 25 October 1996.

89 E.O. Wright, *Interrogating Inequality* (London, 1994), p. 40.

90 A.M. Shaikh and E.A. Tonak, *Measuring the Wealth of Nations* (Cambridge, 1994), pp. 146–51.

91 R. Brenner, 'Uneven Development and the Long Downturn', *New Left Review*, 229 (1998), p. 3.

92 E.O. Wright, *Class Counts* (Cambridge, 1997) is a major attempt systematically to apply an exploitation-based

theory of class to a sample of contemporary capitalist societies.

93 Rawls, *Theory of Justice*, pp. 312, 313.
94 Commission of Social Justice, *The Justice Gap*, pp. 13, 43. See the critique in Cohen, 'Back to Socialist Basics', pp. 37–41.
95 D. Miller, 'What Kind of Equality Should the Left Pursue?', in Franklin, ed., *Equality*, pp. 89, 91. See also B. Williams, 'Forward to Basics', ibid., pp. 51–3, and Miller, *Principles of Social Justice*, ch. 7.
96 Miller, 'What Kind of Equality', p. 92.
97 There is an important account of responsibility in Scanlon, *What We Owe to Each Other*, ch. 6.
98 D. Miller, *Market, State, and Community* (Oxford, 1989), pp. 157, 162.
99 Elsewhere Miller acknowledges this: ibid., pp. 146–50.
100 Ibid., p. 174.
101 In considering Miller's arguments I have benefited from reading an unpublished manuscript by G.A. Cohen, 'David Miller on Market Socialism and Distributive Justice', October 1989.
102 F.A. von Hayek, *The Constitution of Liberty* (London, 1960), p. 94. See Miller, *Principles of Social Justice*, pp. 182–9, for a wholly unpersuasive critique of Hayek.
103 Miller, *Market, State, and Community*, p. 172 n. 30.
104 Marx, 'Critique of the Gotha Programme', pp. 86, 87.
105 Marx, *Capital*, I, pp. 298–300.
106 See P. Stephens, *Politics and the Pound* (London, 1997), ch. 10.
107 For a critical discussion of the fashionable concept of 'risk society', see A. Callinicos, *Social Theory* (Cambridge, 1999), pp. 299–305.
108 Miller, *Market, State, and Community*, pp. 195, 197, 199.
109 E. Balibar, ' "Droits de l'homme" et "droits du citoyen": La Dialectique moderne de l'égalité et de la liberté', *Actuel Marx*, 8 (1990), p. 31.
110 See, for example, R. Rorty, *Contingency, Irony, and Solidarity* (Cambridge, 1989).

111   Marx, 'Critique of the Gotha Programme', pp. 86–7.
112   Sen, *Inequality Reexamined*, p. 121.
113   N. Fraser, 'From Redistribution to Recognition?', *New Left Review*, 212 (1995), pp. 70, 71.
114   Ibid., 72.
115   See esp. I.M. Young, 'Unruly Categories: A Critique of Nancy Fraser's Dual Systems Theory', *New Left Review*, 222 (1997), and N. Fraser, 'A Rejoinder to Iris Young', ibid., 223 (1997).
116   It is important to be clear that stressing the interaction between injustices of distribution and of recognition implies no claim about explanatory priority. In other words, to affirm that, say, racial oppression involves economic deprivations is not necessarily also to affirm that these deprivations (or the tendency for them to occur) causally or functionally *explain* racial oppression. There is, however, an important sense in which I believe the latter claim is true: see A. Callinicos, *Race and Class* (London, 1993), and 'History, Exploitation, and Oppression', *Imprints*, 2 (1997).
117   J. Butler, 'Merely Cultural', *New Left Review*, 227 (1998), and N. Fraser, 'Heterosexism, Misrecognition and Capitalism: A Reply to Judith Butler', ibid., 228 (1998).
118   Fraser, 'From Redistribution to Recognition', pp. 86–91.
119   Anne Phillips offers a judicious discussion of these issues in *Which Equalities Matter?* (Cambridge, 1999).
120   Barry, *Equality as Impartiality*, pp. 3ff, and Scanlon, *What We Owe to Each Other*, ch. 7.

Chapter 4   Equality and captalism

1   J. Roemer, *Equality of Opportunity* (Cambridge, MA, 1998), pp. 74–83.
2   A. Ryan, 'Britain: Recycling the Third Way', *Dissent*, Spring 1999, p. 77. See also W.G. Runciman, 'Diary', *London Review of Books*, 10 December 1998, p. 33.

3 For two classic accounts, see G. Dangerfield, *The Strange Death of Liberal England* (London, 1935), and R.C.K. Ensor, *England 1870–1914* (Oxford, 1936), chs XII and XIII. Peter Clarke has written several more emollient, but still illuminating studies of the New Liberalism, notably *Lancashire and the New Liberalism* (Cambridge, 1971) and *Liberals and Social Democrats* (Cambridge, 1978).

4 D. Cannadine, *The Decline and Fall of the British Aristocracy* (London, 1990), pp. 69–70.

5 P. Stephens, 'Who Gives a Damn for the Blessed Poor?', *Financial Times*, 9 April 1997.

6 R. Gott, 'The Drive to Intervene', *Guardian*, 20 May 1999.

7 See A. Callinicos, 'Barbarity and Hypocrisy: The Ideology of Humanitarian Intervention', in T. Ali, ed., *Masters of the Universe?* (London, 2000).

8 S. Brittan, 'A Good "Liberal" Budget', *Financial Times*, 19 March 1998.

9 D. Piachaud, 'Wealth by Stealth', *Guardian*, *Society* supplement, 1 September 1999.

10 S. White, 'What Do Egalitarians Want?', in J. Franklin, *Equality* (London, 1997), pp. 70–1.

11 G. Brown, 'The Politics of Potential: A New Agenda for Labour', in D. Miliband, ed., *Reinventing the Left* (Cambridge, 1994), p. 114.

12 Ibid., p. 116.

13 J. Rogers and W. Streeck, 'Productive Solidarities', in Miliband, ed., *Reinventing the Left*. For a critical assessment of New Labour economic thinking, see N. Thompson, 'Supply Side Socialism', *New Left Review*, 216 (1996).

14 HM Treasury, *Tackling Poverty and Extending Opportunity*, March 1999, pp. 23, 35.

15 Ibid., p. 23.

16 Brown's acceptance of the analytical core of monetarism, including the doctrine of the natural rate of unemployment (though not all its policy prescriptions), is spelled

out in his Mais lecture, 'The Conditions of Full Employment', 19 October 1999, www.hm-treasury.gov.uk.

17 Quoted in P. Clarke, *The Keynesian Revolution in the Making, 1924–1936* (Oxford, 1988), p. 136.

18 'Europe: The Third Way/*Die Neue Mitte* – Tony Blair and Gerhard Schröder', 6 June 1999, www.labour.org.uk, p. 6.

19 Ibid., p. 8.

20 Ibid., p. 12.

21 Ibid., p. 11.

22 G. Brown, Speech to the Labour Party Conference, 27 Sep. 1999, www.lab.org.uk, p. 7 (emphasis added).

23 *Financial Times*, 10 November 1999.

24 Piachaud, 'Wealth by Stealth'.

25 *Tackling Poverty and Extending Opportunity*, p. 32.

26 'Europe: The Third Way/*Die Neue Mitte*', p. 9.

27 R. Kuttner, 'Don't Forget the Demand Side', in Miliband, ed., *Reinventing the Left*, p. 146.

28 E. Luttwak, *Turbo-Capitalism* (London, 1999), pp. 79, 80–1.

29 Ibid., pp. 82, 83.

30 'Europe: The Third Way/*Die Neue Mitte*', pp. 12–13.

31 T. Blair, 'Speech to the Labour Party Conference', 28 September 1999, www.lab.org.uk, pp. 4, 8.

32 It is entirely typical of this ideological climate that the Commission on Social Justice should concede that 'one person's reward can be another person's loss' and, sliding quickly past the case of 'vast rewards for captains of industry', cite in illustration of this truth the high wage-claims that it supposes caused the stagflation of the 1970s: *The Justice Gap* (London, 1993), p. 14. The thought that the captains of industry might bear some responsibility for inequality and poverty cannot be voiced in the contemporary Labour Party.

33 Brown, 'Speech to the Labour Party Conference', pp. 6, 7. Roosevelt's second term (1937–41) in fact saw the New Deal run aground. In particular, the administration's switch, under conservative pressure, from deficit finance

to a balanced budget helped to abort the recovery from the Great Depression and precipitate the 1937–8 recession, '[t]he steepest economic descent in the history of the United States', according to Charles Kindleberger, *The World in Depression 1929–1939* (Harmondsworth, 1987), p. 271. For an interesting contemporary analysis, see J. Strachey, *A Programme for Progress* (London, 1940), Part II.

34 *Financial Times*, 20 July 1999.

35 A. Maddison, *Dynamic Forces in Capitalist Development* (Oxford, 1991), p. 48 and Table 3.2, p. 50.

36 *Financial Times*, 21 December 1996.

37 *OECD Employment Outlook*, June 1999.

38 On Russia's experience of neo-liberalism, see M. Haynes and P. Glatter, 'The Russian Catastrophe', *International Socialism*, 2.81 (1998), and P. Gowan, *The Global Gamble* (London, 1999), ch. 9.

39 *OECD Employment Outlook*, June 1999.

40 See J. Grahl, *After Maastricht* (London, 1997).

41 J.K. Galbraith et al., 'Inequality and Unemployment in Europe: The American Cure', *New Left Review*, 237 (1999).

42 I am indebted for the general formulation that follows to some remarks of Perry Anderson's: see 'The German Question', *London Review of Books*, 7 January 1999, p. 16.

43 W. Hutton, *The State We're In* (London, 1995), and L. Elliott and D. Atkinson, *The Age of Insecurity* (London, 1998).

44 For analyses of the East Asian and Russian crashes, see A. Callinicos, 'World Capitalism at the Abyss', *International Socialism*, 2.81 (1998), and Gowan, *Global Gamble*, ch. 6. A useful theoretical analysis is provided by M. Itoh and C. Lapavitsas, *Political Economy of Money and Finance* (London, 1999).

45 *Financial Times*, 21 June 1999.

46 Stratfor, 'World Bank Reverses Position on Financial Controls and on Malaysia', *Global Intelligence Update: Weekly Analysis*, 20 September 1999, www.stratfor.com.

47 *Guardian*, 10 October 1998.

48 J. Plender, 'Taming Wild Money', *Financial Times*, 20 October 1998.

49 M. Wolf, 'No Magic Potion', *Financial Times*, 12 May 1999.

50 See, for example, M. Wolf, 'Watch Out for the Fireworks', *Financial Times*, 27 January 1999. The highly unstable set of financial imbalances sustaining the American boom is carefully analysed in two Phillips & Drew research papers by Bill Martin and Wynne Godley, 'America and the World Economy' (December 1998) and 'America's New Era' (October 1999).

51 For a brief exposition of Marx's crisis theory, see A. Callinicos, *The Revolutionary Ideas of Karl Marx* (London, 1983), ch. 6. Useful signposts in the vast literature on this subject include C. Harman, *Explaining the Crisis* (rev. edn, London, 1999), J. Weeks, *Capital and Exploitation* (London, 1981), M.C. Howard and J.E. King, *A History of Marxian Economics* (2 vols, London, 1989, 1992), and S. Clarke, *Marx's Theory of Crisis* (London, 1994).

52 R. Brenner, 'Uneven Development and the Long Downturn: The Advanced Capitalist Economies from Boom to Stagnation, 1950–1998', *New Left Review*, 229 (1998), p. 7. Another recent major study that focuses on the behaviour of the rate of profit is G. Duménil and D. Lévy, *La Dynamique du capital* (Paris, 1996). For a critical assessment of Brenner's article, see A. Callinicos, 'Capitalism, Competition, and Profits', *Historical Materialism*, 4 (1999).

53 Callinicos, 'Capitalism at the Abyss', pp. 21–4.

54 United Nations Development Programme, *Human Development Report 1999* (New York, 1999), p. 40.

55 M. Albert, *Capitalism against Capitalism* (London, 1993) offers the most general statement of the stakeholder case, though it has, of course, informed Hutton's writings. For a critique, see A. Callinicos, 'Betrayal and Discontent: New Labour under Blair', *International Socialism*, 2.72 (1996), pp. 5–13.

56 B. Barry, 'The Attractions of Basic Income', in J. Franklin, ed., *Equality* (London, 1997).

57 R. Van Parijs and R. Van Der Veen, 'A Capitalist Road to Communism', in P. Van Parijs, *Marxism Recycled* (Cambridge, 1993), p. 163.

58 Id., 'Universal Grants versus Socialism', in Van Parijs, *Marxism Recycled*, pp. 178, 179.

59 Ibid., p. 206 n. 4.

60 *Financial Times*, 6 September 1999. There is an excellent critique of the thesis of the end of work in M. Husson, 'Fin du travail ou réduction de sa durée?', *Actuel Marx*, 26 (1999).

61 Van Parijs and Van Der Veen, 'Universal Grants versus Socialism', p. 189.

62 *Financial Times*, 13 March 1999.

63 Barry, 'The Attractions of Basic Income', p. 163.

64 See E.O. Wright, 'Why Something like Socialism is Necessary for the Transition to Something like Communism', in id., *Interrogating Inequality* (London, 1994).

65 *Libération*, 3 October 1998.

66 *Financial Times*, 7 June 1997.

67 J. Wolfreys, 'Class Struggles in France', *International Socialism*, 84 (1999).

68 See, for example, J. Rawls, *A Theory of Justice* (rev. edn, Oxford, 1999), pp. xiv–xvi, and R. Dworkin, 'Liberalism', in M. Sandel, ed., *Liberalism and Its Critics* (Oxford, 1984), pp. 68–9.

69 G.A. Cohen, 'Back to Socialist Basics', in Franklin, ed., *Equality*, p. 37.

70 Id., *Self-Ownership, Freedom, and Equality* (Cambridge, 1995), pp. 259, 262.

71 P. Devine, *Democracy and Economic Planning* (Cambridge, 1988). For a somewhat broader discussion of the issues raised in this and preceding paragraphs, see A. Callinicos, *The Revenge of History* (Cambridge, 1991).

72 T. Nagel, *Equality and Partiality* (New York, 1991), p. 4.

73 Ibid., pp. 90, 91, 124.

74 Ibid., p. 125.

75 The philosophical underpinnings of Nagel's position will be found in *The View from Nowhere* (New York, 1986).

76 G.A. Cohen, 'Incentives, Inequality, and Community', in G.B. Peterson, ed., *The Tanner Lectures on Human Values*, XIII (Salt Lake City, 1992), pp. 269–70. See chapter 3 above.

77 Cohen, *Self-Ownership, Freedom, and Equality*, p. 262. See also id., 'Back to Socialist Basics', pp. 35–7.

78 See Wolfreys, 'Class Struggles in France', and S. Béroud et al., *Le Mouvement social en France* (Paris, 1998). For a discussion of some of the intellectual consequences, see A. Callinicos, 'Social Theory Put to the Test of Politics: Pierre Bourdieu and Anthony Giddens', *New Left Review*, 236 (1999), pp. 85–102.

79 *Michael Moore's Newsletter*, 7 December 1999, www. michaelmoore.com.

80 G.B. Shaw, *The Intelligent Woman's Guide to Socialism and Capitalism* (London, 1928), p. 385.

81 Cohen, 'Incentives, Inequality, and Community', e.g. pp. 307–10.

Index